Growing a Healthy Workforce:

Leading in the Eight Dimensions of Workplace Wellness

Andrew L. McCart, PhD

Dear Tyler,

Thank you so much for serving on our advisory board! May your healthiest & happiest days be yet to come!

— Andrew

Growing a Healthy Workforce: Leading in the Eight
Dimensions of Organizational Wellness

ISBN: 1720551596
ISBN-13: 978-1720551591

DEDICATION

To Deven, for growing a healthy me.

The Parable of the Bamboo Plant

Growing a bamboo plant is an exercise in patience, perseverance, and long-term thinking. Once the seed is sewn by an eager landscaper, it must be watered and fertilized for an entire year. When nothing grows above the surface of the ground, the landscaper must water and fertilize it for the entire second year. Again, there is no evidence of the efforts that have been poured into the anticipation of future. And the story is the same for the third and fourth year; watering and fertilizing, hoping and wondering—with no evidence of success.

But, in the fifth year, the miraculous and unbelievable happens. Within a few short weeks, the bamboo plant grows <u>90 feet</u>. Nature puts on a display of its power and it turns the natural order on its head. In contrast, growing trees produce results in one season, other crops produce fruit after a few months, and a flower often blooms even faster. The bamboo plant, however, doesn't show up until the fifth year. And then, in a few weeks, it shoots up toward the sun.

Of course, the bamboo plant did not grow up in a few week. It took every day of effort during the five years. If the landscaper would have stopped at any point during those years, the plant would have died in the ground. If friends, neighbors, bosses, coworkers, or even well-meaning family members would have seen the landscaper during those five years, they would have likely accused him of wasting his time on something that is not bearing visible fruit.

Growing a Healthy Workforce and Leading in the Eight Dimensions of Workplace Wellness are like growing the miraculous bamboo plant. It will take years of effort before there is a clear ROI on the balance sheet; yet the costs will be seen today. People won't understand. Employees will leave to find other jobs after years of investing in them.

We have to do it anyway. What if the employees stay? We will want them to be healthy. Most importantly, it's the right thing to do. Treating employees as though their health is very important sends a message about how the company feels about them.

Don't give up in persuading your bosses or financial officers that this is a worthwhile investment. Don't give up in convincing your coworkers and employees that they should make healthier choices. Don't give up in holding informational meetings and providing healthy living tips. They will thank you one day. And, if they don't, it's still the right thing to do.

CONTENTS

ACKNOWLEDGMENTS

This book is the culmination of my PhD coursework and dissertation at the University of Louisville. Setting and achieving a goal that spans over six years is something that goes beyond the ability of one person. Like many other adult students, I have made it this far only with the support of family, friends, colleagues, my employer, and the instructors at the School of Public Health and Information Sciences.

In my family, Deven, Carol Sue, and Larry McCart have encouraged me all along; especially in the final stages of setting dissertation goals and even polishing the manuscript on our honeymoon! Eliza, Louis, Liam, and Teddy Gordner made me an uncle and caused me to want to be someone to look up to. Chuck and Jenny Harrison and Jorge and Lauren Pazmino are the best in-laws I could ask for; I hit the lottery with them. Thank you for your love and support. I am grateful and blessed to have all of you in my life.

Sometime during year two of my six year PhD study, I was spending a lot of time with my great friend Jason Akin. He helped me get focused on my studies and on my life. I'm forever grateful for his advice and influence.

The dissertation committee that has guided this research is, to me, an all-star cast of professionals in academia and industry. Their combined experience has been helpful and humbling during this process. My advisor, Dr. Susan Olson Allen, has been very supportive and patient during the process, especially during our periods of weekly meetings and when my IRB approval seemed to take more time than I thought it should. Dr. Robert Esterhay was helpful in the all stages of my degree, teaching the first class in which I was enrolled, and helping guide this dissertation along the way. Dr. Dave Roelfs really helped the process by joining the team from outside the School of Public Health and providing invaluable insight in the qualitative aspects of the study. Dr. James Taylor provided extremely helpful insight from the perspective of industry and academia.

I must also acknowledge students that walked this road with me and helped by providing humor, encouragement, and strategic insights at different stages of the degree. Drs. Jennifer Forristal, Robin Weiss, and Steve Zimmerman became, not only examples that this degree could be completed, but they also became friends.

Thank you to all those that participated as interviewees in this study; I wish you health and wellness for all of your days.

FOREWORD

Employers are looking for strategies to help them become a healthier workplace. Many employers see the expense of paying for an unhealthy workforce and they are looking to limit these expenses. The purpose of the study is to determine the state of workplace wellness activities in employees' words. In my region, this is even more important due to the poor health statuses of Indiana and Kentucky, 39th and 45th, respectively, this study is significant for a number of stakeholders in our area.

The purpose of this case study is to understand the state of health and wellness of organizations in Southern Indiana and Greater Louisville, according to the Centers for Disease Control Health Scorecard (CDC, 2014). Participants were first given the Centers for Disease Control Health Scorecard (CDC HSC) to develop a consistent quantitative baseline. The CDC HSC is a 125 question, 264-point survey that covers a diverse set of work place wellness initiatives. During the survey, participants were encouraged to elaborate on any aspect of the CDC HSC, such as organizational structure, tobacco control, physical activity, or any of the other categories included. Participants were then asked a series of open-ended interview questions to explore the ways they are, or are not, addressing the health and wellness in their workplace.

The population from the study includes organizations from Southern Indiana and Greater Louisville. The results of the interviews were transcribed and compared to themes in the literature for patterns, themes, and outliers. Twenty-five organizations were included in the study, including a sole proprietorship that shares the thoughts of a mid-20s entrepreneur in the technology industry. The individuals interviewed have a variety of roles in their organizations, so it is assumed they represent the majority of the workforce in their knowledge of the wellness programs. The pilot study focused on managers and human resources personnel and the researcher felt they were biased in their knowledge of the programs. So, the next twenty organizations focused on employees that did create the wellness programs, as the leaders and HR managers in the pilot study did.

The organizations vary in size, by industry, for-profit versus non-profit, and in the positions of the respondents. The interview material is presented by sharing the data from high, middle, and low-scoring organizations.

Part 1: Introduction

1. THE $5.7 TRILLION QUESTION

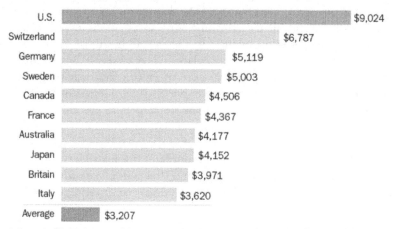

BIGGEST HEALTH CARE SPENDERS
Countries with largest per capita health care expenditures, 2015

U.S.	$9,024
Switzerland	$6,787
Germany	$5,119
Sweden	$5,003
Canada	$4,506
France	$4,367
Australia	$4,177
Japan	$4,152
Britain	$3,971
Italy	$3,620
Average	$3,207

SOURCE: Organization for Economic Co-operation and Development   TRIBUNE NEWS SERVICE

$5.7 Trillion is the projected amount the United States will spend on healthcare in 2026, according to the Centers for Medicare and Medicaid Services.

This chapter begins with a background to the topic of workplace wellness. According to the CDC, workplace wellness programs are defined as "a coordinated and comprehensive set of health promotion and protection strategies implemented at the worksite that includes programs, policies, benefits, environmental supports, and links to the surrounding community designed to encourage the health and safety of all employees" (CDC, 2016) The problem statement, the purpose of the study and the significance of the study follow. Next, Part 2 looks at organizational supports, Part 3 looks at the other seven dimensions of workplace wellness, and Part 4 wraps up the book with best practices, a sole proprietor case study and future research.

"Employers' health costs are projected to rise 6.5% a one year."

Workplace health and wellness is an increasingly significant cost for organizations in the United States. This chapter outlines a dissertation that will address the problems an unhealthy work place experiences and discusses strategies used in relation to the overall health of employees and the cost of healthcare in the workplace. The costs of healthcare are a significant component in the total cost of labor. According to the U.S. Department of Health and Human Services, (U.S. Department of Health and Human Services, 2014), the average single person premium in the U.S. in 2014 was $5,832, with an employee contribution of $1,234 and an average employer contribution of $4,598. In more unhealthy environments, the cost of healthcare is an even larger burden. For instance, on the macro-scale, the Centers for Disease Control and Prevention state that obesity and other chronic health problems have tremendous costs. (CDC, 2016)

"Chronic health problems cause employees to miss about 450 million more days of work each year than healthy workers, at a cost of $153 billion in lost productivity each year." (CDC, 2016)

Organizations need to adjust with these increases in health care costs quickly because the high cost of healthcare is on the rise. Employers' health costs are projected to rise 6.5% for 2016 (Miller, 2015). This increase corresponds with a study conducted by the US Department of Health and Human Services (U. S. Department of Health and Human Services, 2007) projected that U.S. health care spending would grow from $2 trillion, in 2005, which represents 16% of Gross Domestic Product (GDP) to $4 trillion in 2015, or 20% of GDP. These costs seem staggering when compared to ten years ago. If the next ten years continue at this pace, the health of the workforce will become one of the top expenses for the nation. According to the Bureau of Labor Statistics, (U.S. Department of Labor, 2016b) the average cost for health insurance benefits is 7.6% of total compensation, with Union Labor experiencing health insurance benefits of 12.6% of total compensation.

MEDICAL COST RETURN ON INVESTMENT

The ability to control and reduce this expense can be a competitive advantage for companies operating domestically and internationally. In 2010, the CDC (CDC, 2014) found:

"Medical costs return on investment (ROI) to be $3.27 for every dollar spent and the absenteeism ROI to be $2.73 for every dollar spent," for a total of $6.00 returned on each dollar invested.

This level of savings may be a trend that has the potential to reverse the runaway healthcare costs in the United States. A six times return on investment can compete with many other options for investing cash on hand, including most stocks, bonds, and mutual funds.

In many industries, international competition does not directly face the same cost of employee health and wellness that U.S. companies face. All of Europe has enacted some form of national health insurance in their history and many Asian countries, including China, Hong Kong, India, Singapore and Taiwan provide public healthcare. According to the Peter G. Peterson Foundation (Foundation, 2016), the United States spends more than twice the average per capita on healthcare spending as other developed countries, at $8,713 per person compared to the average of $3,453 per person in the other Organization for Economic Cooperation and Development (OEDC) countries. OECD countries include Italy, the U.K., Japan, Australia, France, Canada, Germany, Sweden, Switzerland, and others. Since foreign competitors do not have the high healthcare expenses that the United States companies have, they can reduce the cost of the production of their goods or services and offer prices that are more competitive.

HISTORY OF EMPLOYER SPONSORED HEALTHCARE

There are several reasons why costs are so much higher in the U.S. First, the history of employer-sponsored health care set the stage for the U.S. economy to experience the current workplace wellness costs. United

States' employers began to assume responsibility for employee health care in the 1940s and 50s when the Internal Revenue Service ruled that employer-sponsored healthcare should be tax free (Blumberg, 2009) . The 1942 Stabilization Act created by Congress limited wage increases during wartime. The point was to combat inflation, but the effect was that employers began giving more generous health benefits as a way to attract and retain talent (Toland, 2014). In the 1940s and 1950s, healthcare coverage was much less expensive than it is today. For instance, in 1960, total health care expenditures, as a percentage of GDP was 5.1%, compared to 2010 when it was 17.6% (Allin, 2012). This threefold increase in 50 years demonstrates the importance of addressing this problem on a macroeconomic scale.

Another reason for the dramatic increase in work place health care costs is the rise of chronic disease. Chronic disease management is one of the major factors that is driving up the cost of healthcare for employers in the US (De Libero, 2013). The CDC (2014) states that 75% of the nation's $2.2 trillion medical care costs are due to chronic diseases in the population. Chronic diseases include heart disease, stroke, cardiovascular disease, obesity, diabetes, and diseases related to tobacco use. Heart disease and stroke are responsible for 33% of reported deaths each year (Roger et al., 2012). Cardiovascular Disease is responsible for 17% of US healthcare expenditures and that will increase dramatically as the nation ages (Heidenreich et al., 2011). In 2008, obesity cost $147 billion annually (Finkelstein, Trogdon, Cohen, & Dietz, 2009). In 2007, the Department of Health and Human Services estimated diabetes costs at $174 billion annually in direct healthcare costs and indirect costs, such as absenteeism and disability (CDC, 2011). The costs of tobacco use are around $192.8 billion per year (CDC, 2008).

WHERE SHOULD LEADERS START?

The complex and broad nature of workplace wellness makes it a potentially troublesome and broad topic for employers. Employers need to be cautious in not only finding an effective workplace wellness program but also ensuring that they remain legal in designing their programs. Employers that are creating wellness programs need to examine the legal aspects and further emphasize the need to be effective, legal, simple, and gain participation from employees.

When trying to understand workplace wellness programs, it is important to understand what employers feel make a successful program. Historically, financial incentives and participation in wellness programs have been the primary measures of success. (Dee W. Edington, 2015) Financial incentives or participation only demonstrate short term results and do not really look at health markers or behavioral change over time.

The problem of workplace wellness is further complicated because employers do not always know how to begin to improve the health of their workforce, so little is done to decrease cost. A simple Google search of 'workplace wellness' returns over 1.2 million results. The data that is found from a search this broad can report conflicting information that reports anything from a six-times return on invest to a negative ROI. This lack of knowledge in work place wellness can cause leaders to feel overwhelmed when trying to address this growing problem. Leaders see the total health costs going up at an unbridled rate, but also can also feel conflicted in taking action because they see the upfront costs of any kind of workplace wellness programs. Without sufficient knowledge of the ROI, which is not realized until the medium to long term, leaders may be leery of investing in an unknown and expensive preventative program.

Furthermore, even if they believe the program is worthwhile, their organization may not have the labor or time to research and implement a program. The above factors make the workplace a natural fit to improve the overall health of the population in the United States, as a large percentage of individuals are employed. In June of 2016, unemployment was just below 5%, according to the Bureau of Labor Statistics (U.S. Department of Labor, 2016c). Unemployment rates in Indiana and Kentucky agree with these national averages at 5.0% and 5.1%, respectively (U.S. Department of Labor, 2016a). Because a financial stake exists for employers, they may be eager consumers for this information to improve the health and wellness of their workforce.

LEGAL CONCERNS OF WELLNESS PROGRAMS

The information overload felt by organizational leaders is compounded by the need for any workplace wellness program to be legal. As mentioned previously, employers need help sifting through the information and finding a program that provides results, is implementable, and is within the bounds of multiple federal policies. The fact that there are legal ramifications for incorrectly conducting wellness programs means that employers may require assistance in interpreting the law. The Employee Retirement Income Security Act (ERISA), the Americans with Disabilities Act (ADA), the Genetic Information Nondiscrimination Act (GINA), the Health Insurance Portability and Accountability Act (HIPPA), and the Patient Protection and Affordable Care Act (PPACA) all have provisions that prevent discrimination based on health conditions and the collecting and sharing of information. ERISA prohibits group plans from discriminating against an individual because of their health status (Pollitz, 2016). According to the Equal Employment Opportunity Commission (EEOC), the ADA does not allow employers to discriminate based on disability and prohibits employers from gathering medical information from applicants, but employers can do so as part of a voluntary work place wellness program (Commission, 2016b).

GINA prevents employers from making employment decisions using genetic information and it restricts them from requesting, requiring, or purchasing genetic information in most cases. The EEOC states that a wellness program must be "reasonably designed" so that it promotes health or prevents disease and cannot merely shift the burden of cost to employees upon the basis of their health status (Commission, 2016a). HIPPA can also be confusing to employers who are designing workplace wellness programs. According to the Department of Health and Human Services, HIPPA does not apply to employers in their capacity as employers, but can apply to a wellness program that is offered as part of a group health plan (U.S. Department of Health and Human Services, 2012). This study will take HIPPA and the other policy requirements into consideration when making recommendations for programs to implement.

Similarly, the PPACA has restrictions to protect consumers from discriminatory practices by employers and within wellness programs. The PPACA supports "participatory wellness programs" that support health without regard to an employee's individual health status, such as discounts to a fitness center, attendance at a no-cost educational seminar, or participating in a health risk assessment which does not require action on the employees' part (U.S. Department of Labor, 2014). The PPACA rules allow for nondiscriminatory rewards based on "health-contingent wellness programs." These programs can be within the PPACA guidelines if they encourage employees to meet certain health goals, such as to abstain or decrease their tobacco use or meet certain weight or cholesterol levels (U.S. Department of Labor, 2014). The PPACA protects consumers by ensuring that wellness programs follow certain rules. Programs must not be overly burdensome to employees, they must reasonably improve health or prevent disease for employees, and programs must be designed for all "similarly situated individuals"(U.S. Department of Labor, 2014). This study investigates aspects of the legalese of these various acts for employers.

Wellness programs also need to be conducted within the rule of the law in order to avoid discrimination. If leadership is not involved from the top-down, they may not be aware of certain weight loss competitions, exercise promotion, or activities. It is possible that wellness programs can be discriminatory; employees can collect biometrics incorrectly, or be in conflict with five or more federal acts. Programs must adhere to various laws regarding employees' health and wellness and the sharing of information, such as The Employee Retirement Income Security Act (ERISA), the Americans with Disabilities Act (ADA), the Genetic Information Nondiscrimination Act (GINA), the Health Insurance Portability and Accountability Act (HIPPA), and the Patient Protection and Affordable Care Act (PPACA).

Wellness programs that provide rewards for completing a participatory health risk assessment are the most common type of wellness program in the United States. (Pomeranz, 2015) The incentives provided by these programs can raise concerns about their voluntary nature and the Americans with Disabilities Act of 1990 states that employers cannot require health-related inquiries and exams. (Pomeranz, 2015). Information gathered from a health risk assessment, such as weight, blood pressure, or blood lipid levels or any other biometric data must be voluntary because it can determine health status, physical activity, or smoking activity. (Mello & Rosenthal, 2008) All of this data must be handled in compliance with HIPPA, the ADA, GINA, and be treated as confidential and separate from personnel records. (EEOC, 2011) Leadership needs to be involved in the initial phases of a health risk assessments to ensure they are lawfully conducted.

PROVIDE MULTIPLE WELLNESS PROGRAMS BASED ON EMPLOYEES' HEALTH STATUS

According to Goetzel (Goetzel & Ozminkowski, 2008), worksite health programs focus on three different types of activities. Different lanes or categories of populations can be similar as the slow, fast, and carpool lanes on the highway. A 16-wheel tractor trailer is going to go slower, it needs to be in the slow lane so it doesn't slow down the faster cars and car pool drivers. Similarly, employees with varying health need to be treated differently.

1.) HEALTHY POPULATIONS: The first type of programs are primary prevention efforts and focus on generally healthy populations, as well as options for workers who do not focus on their health, but can prevent diseases if they participate in the program (Goetzel & Ozminkowski, 2008). These individuals can benefit from participating in exercise and fitness classes, proper nutrition, weight and stress classes, vaccine preventable diseases, and understanding the benefits of only engaging in low to moderate alcohol intake. Primary prevention efforts can also help employees who may seem healthy or believe they are healthy, but who may not be aware that they have risk factors for cardiovascular disease (CVD). (Wong et al., 2007)

2.) HIGH RISK FOR POOR HEALTH: The second type of wellness programs can promote health to a second group of individuals that are a high risk for poor health. These individuals are at risk for poor health because they may smoke, work sedentary jobs, drink alcohol excessively, practice unsafe sex, or experience high levels of stress. Encouraging this group to participate in regular physical activity can be extremely important to worksite health. Habitually sedentary individuals have significantly higher rates of CVD and low levels of physical fitness are among the strongest determinants of CVD and all-cause mortality. (Kodama and Saito, 2009) Low levels of fitness are also associated with higher health care costs and even small improvements in physical fitness habits can have a major impact on health outcomes. (Weiss, Froelicher, Myers, & Heidenreich, 2004)

This second group often has biometric values that are abnormally high, specifically pertaining to blood pressure, diabetes, obesity, or cholesterol. (Goetzel, 2008) Health promotion in the work place can reach this group by focusing on hypertension screenings, smoking cessation, weight loss education, and/or helping employees overcome financial barriers to healthier choices, such as obtaining medicine to control their biometric values. Weight loss education can be extremely important because nutrition habits in the United States are well below the Department of Health and Human Services and other widely recognized standards. (Abbot and Byrd, 2007). For instance, the Nurses' Health Study found that only 12.7% of 84,000 individuals surveyed met minimal standards for a healthy diet. (Stampfer, Hu, & Willett, 2000)

3.) EXISTING CONDITIONS: The third group of health promotion activities that Goetzel identifies is considered disease management for the segment of the population with an existing condition. These programs are directed at individuals with existing ailments, such as "asthma, diabetes, cardiovascular disease, cancers, musculoskeletal disorders, and depression." (Goetzel, 2008) The aim of these types of interventions is to slow down the disease or improve the condition through better adherence to their clinical protocols.

Positive changes in this third group can yield big benefits for the organization. The Mayo Clinic proceedings tell of a study of 58% of employees who were "high risk" at the beginning of a wellness program that converted to low risk after a simple and targeted intervention program. (Arena et al., 2013) After the study, significant improvements were seen in body fat content, blood pressure, plasma lipid levels, depression, anxiety, hostility, somatization, quality of life, and total health scores.(Milani & Lavie, 2009) These programs also need to encourage communication among patients, their family, physicians, and other health care providers.

WHAT GOALS DO EMPLOYERS HAVE FOR WELLENSS PROGRAMS?

In studying effective wellness programs, it is helpful to understand what executives hope to achieve through wellness initiatives. A survey of the literature reveals a long list of hopes and wishes that employers want in wellness programs. Goetzel et al provide a very comprehensive list of the expectations employers may place on their wellness programs:

1. "Make workers aware of their health and how being in good health improves quality of life.

2. Workers should take 'ownership' of their behaviors and be accountable for health and cost outcomes.

3. High participation and active involvement in these programs. People should take advantage of the many programs offered.

4. Employees should lose weight, stop smoking, exercise more often, eat a healthy diet, better manage their stress levels, and generally adopt healthy habits.

5. Medical claims costs should go down. The company should experience a lower incidence of certain diseases linked to behaviors like diabetes, heart disease, cancer, chronic obstructive pulmonary disease (COPD), musculoskeletal disorders, and stroke.

6. Workers will be absent less often, disability costs will be controlled, accidents will be avoided, and injury rates should drop sharply.

7. These programs will attract the best talent—and turnover rates will be reduced because we are the employer of choice in the community.

8. Workers will perform at higher levels—they will be happier, have more energy, and produce better results for our company.

9. Establish a culture of health and well-being, where every worker feels valued and important to the enterprise—this will inspire greater loyalty and a high level of engagement.

10. The program will produce a positive return-on-investment (ROI) for the company—for every dollar spent, two or three will be saved."(Goetzel et al., 2014)

This list of expectations is very wide and far ranging. It is unlikely that a single employer will receive all of these benefits from their programs. The list helps to demonstrate the variety of hopes that management place on wellness programs and the unrealistic approach they may use to determine wellness programs' success or failure. For employers to achieve these results, they need to be sure to reach the most high-risk (and hard to reach) individuals that use the greatest percentage of health care dollars. (Joslin, Lowe, & Peterson, 2006)

This list of expectations causes one to wonder how employers can create a comprehensive and robust program that meets all of these expectations. Some programs only focus on one aspect of health promotion or disease prevention. Those are not capable of achieving even half of the list of ten items above. Although it is difficult to know where to start, the literature suggests that managers may be able to focus on obesity, as health spending is reportedly "36% higher in obese adults under the age of sixty-five than in normal weight adults." (Thorpe, Florence, Howard, & Joski, 2004) Most of this higher spending is due to "treatments for diabetes, hyperlipidemia, and heart disease." (Thorpe et al., 2004)

COMPREHENSIVE WELLNESS PROGRAMS

Healthy People 2010 provides guidance through a list of five attributes of a comprehensive workplace health program:

1. "Health education, focused on skill development and lifestyle behavior change along with information dissemination and awareness building.

2. Supportive social and physical environments, reflecting the organization's expectations regarding healthy behaviors and implementing policies promoting healthy behaviors.

3. Integration of the worksite program into the organization's benefits, human resources infrastructure, and environmental health and safety initiatives.

4. Links between health promotion and related programs like employee assistance.

5. Screenings followed by counseling and education on how to best use medical services for necessary follow-up." (U. D. o. H. a. H. Services, 2000)

COMMON QUESTIONS EXPLORED IN THIS STUDY

1. Which workplace wellness activities do employers engage in readily and what are their perceived costs and benefits for engaging in those activities?

2. Which workplace wellness activities have low employer participation and what are their perceived costs and benefits for not engaging in those activities?

3. Which workplace wellness activities are most effective based on the evidence-based literature?

4. What features of organizational structure encourage employees to engage in healthy behavior and what are the costs and benefits of those features?

5. How do the organizations in this study compare to the findings of average scores in the CDC HSC validation study?

2. WHY DOES THIS MATTER?

"A study including 56 organizations concluded that workplace wellness programs had "25%-30% lower medical or absenteeism expenditures than non-participants."

Policy makers at the local, regional, and national level are also seeking ways to reduce the rapidly growing cost of health in the United States. In recent years, the Patient Protection and Affordable Care Act has brought national attention to this topic, seeking changes and threatening penalties, but providing no real direction in the best way to make these changes for employees. The national statistics of health care costs versus other developed nations and as a percentage of GDP show that the U.S. is spending double the amount on healthcare as other developed nations for similar or worse health outcomes (Davis, 2014). If employers have information on implementing wellness initiatives in their environment, they can do their part to lower the runaway expenses of an unhealthy culture.

Successful pioneers and leaders of workplace wellness have seen remarkable benefits. This demonstrates the significance of more study and dissemination of work place wellness knowledge. One case study of fourteen organizations, conducted by the California Department of Public Health, touts a number of benefits on their examination of "Creating a Culture of Wellness in the Worksite Environment" (California Department of Public Health, 2015). This study saw employees eating more fresh foods, participating in group movement and exercise classes, installing air filters, offering on-site gyms, health education workshops, and many other programs (California Department of Public Health, 2015).

In 2005, a study including 56 organizations concluded that workplace wellness programs had "25%-30% lower medical or absenteeism expenditures than non-participants" (Chapman, 2012). A review in Health Affairs found that medical costs return on investment (ROI) "to be $3.27 for every dollar spent and the absenteeism ROI to be $2.73 for every dollar spent"(Baicker, Cutler, & Zirui, 2010). The results experienced in workplace wellness in isolated geographies can help promote workplace wellness and financial savings on a larger scale.

This study is also significant because the CDC health scorecard is a relatively new tool and there has not been much research on the usage of the scorecard since its inception in 2012. The primary literature on the CDC Worksite Health Scorecard (HSC) is the article from a team at Emory University, which tested the reliability and validity of the HSC (CDC, 2014). This study has been cited by 7 authors, according to a Google Scholar search on July 25, 2016, which is only three less citations than the 10 cited instances of the HSC itself. The Emory study tested the original HSC at 93 worksites, examining question responses and conducting interviews to refine the instrument for general distribution (CDC, 2014). The purpose of the HSC is to serve as an assessment tool for employers to examine their health promotion programs, to identify gaps, and to develop an effective strategy to implement interventions that address heart disease, stroke, and related chronic conditions. The conclusion of the Emory testing was that their revised version of the HSC "represents one of the few current, comprehensive, and evidence-based worksite tools that have undergone reliability and validity testing and are publicly available for addressing a significant and growing need confronting America's business community" (CDC, 2014).

THE NUDGE THEORY

In addition to the CDC HSC, the study will investigate if the Nudge Theory is relevant in the health and wellness of these organizations. The Nudge Theory will help determine whether employers guide employees to healthier behavior use 'choice architecture'. Choice architecture is a practice of setting up organizational structures to guide the employees to behave in certain ways. Nudge Theory is "any aspect of the choice architecture that alters people's behavior in a predictable way without forbidding any options or significantly changing their economic incentives. To count as a mere nudge, the intervention must be cheap and easy to avoid. Nudges are not mandates. Putting fruit at eye level, hoping that people then choose fruit over unhealthy alternatives, counts as a nudge. Banning junk food does not." (Frank, 2008)

Nudge Theory is relevant because of its application in the public health and workplace wellness arenas around the world. A field study at Google found that placing healthier snacks and beverages closer to employees than unhealthy snacks and beverages increased the consumption of healthy snacks from 12% to 23%. (Baskin et al., 2016). This strategy allowed employers to reduce unhealthy snack consumption in a way that did not create backlash from employees, just by increasing the relative distance to unhealthy choices.

Nudging individuals toward healthier behavior can help overcome the occurrences of mindlessly unhealthy behavior, particularly eating, and other actions that precede conscious thought (Chance, Gorlin, & Dhar, 2014). For instance,

---

An individual may not consciously consume a bucket of popcorn at the movies as part of a well-thought out decision. They likely did not engage in an analysis that they preferred a bucket of buttered popcorn to no popcorn.

The choice was likely made out of habit, the flow of the line from the ticket stand to the concession stand, and the smells and sounds that compelled unconscious processes to choose the popcorn.

Another example of Nudge Theory in public health is in the Japanese approach to obesity. Controlling weight gain is a major consideration for developed nations and the Japanese "maintain a low prevalence relative to other developed countries" (Borovoy & Roberto, 2015). Choice architecture is said to be responsible as the Japanese government nudges society by prescribing optimal body metrics for Japanese citizens and then encourages schools and health insurance organizations to carry out education. For the American workplace, this is an illustration of how organizations set a standard of health and then educate employees on how they can achieve this standard if they desire.

Nudge Theory builds upon two older and more classic theories of economics and sociology. First, the Social Exchange Theory (SET) interprets society as a series of interactions based on estimates of rewards and punishments. According to this view, our interactions with others seek rewards and/or avoid punishments. The SET states that individuals create sets of strategies that they believe will increase the odds in their favor of receiving rewards or avoiding punishments (Witt, 2013). Nudge theory takes this a step further and implies that the process may be below the level of conscious processing. Over time, individuals will learn what behaviors provide rewards by engaging in a variety of behaviors until certain behaviors result in rewards and positive reinforcement. This theory states that all human relationships form with the use of a subjective cost-benefit analysis. Nudging individuals toward certain healthy behaviors will cause individuals to decide that the benefits outweigh the costs for activities that improve their health and wellness.

"The quality of communication and the existence of shared values are positively related to trust between the exchange partners."

Conversely, individuals will not participate in wellness activities for which they perceive the costs outweigh the benefits. One of the basic tenants of Social Exchange Theory (SET) is that trust and loyalty develop over time in relationships and that parties create this by engaging in certain "rules of exchange." (Cropanzano & Mitchell, 2005) Reciprocity is one of the key Social Exchange rules and this can inform employers to make sure that any wellness program needs to be seen as fair by the employees. Young-Ybarra and Wiersema's (Young-Ybarra & Wiersema, 1999) study on SET found that the quality of communication and the existence of shared values "were positively related to trust between the exchange partners". The Nudge Theory states that choice architecture can help build trust because it still leaves the choice up to employees; it only makes healthier choices more readily available than unhealthy choices. This study looks at successful aspects of wellness programs to determine the quality of their communication and values structure.

How do individuals make the determination to healthy choices? This text demonstrates how organizations can encourage individuals to engage in wellness activities, by making the rewards and punishments clear and understandable. To induce employee participation in successful wellness programs, organizations can educate employees on healthier choices. Logical reason can guide employees toward activities where the total benefits outweigh the total costs to the individual, the organization, and society.

"Approval is a 'generalized reinforcer' that can reinforce a wide variety of specialized activities."

The second theory that Nudge Theory builds upon is the Rational Choice Theory (RCT). The RCT argues that social systems organize in ways that structure the alternatives and consequences facing individuals so that they behave rationally. This allows employees to serve their self-interest within the constraints and resources that go with social systems and their status in them. This theory speaks to the structure within organizations that cause the default behavior of individuals to follow certain patterns. Nudge theory states that the organization's leaders decide on a definition of "behaving rationally" and set up the systems that allow employees to serve their self-interests.

The organizational structure can include options that lead to employees engaging in healthy choices. For instance, organizations can drive healthy behavior by creating walking paths, providing healthy nutrition options, instituting safe layouts, or discouraging tobacco use on the property. Conversely, organizations can emerge over time to create unhealthy behavior, such as sedentary or repetitive movement in job positions, "junk food" in vending machines, or acceptance of tobacco usage demonstrated by ashtrays. The research questions determine what types of organizational structures lead to higher scores on the CDC HSC.

Rational Choice Theory holds that individuals pursue their goals efficiently. Individuals may have a great deal of information or no information at all, but they choose the path that they believe will deliver the greatest net rewards based on their understanding of the choices laid before them (Green, 2007). Further, Green and Fox (2007) explain that RCT does not require that the rewards are self-serving in nature. An individual's rewards could be altruism, improvements in their community, or even self-destruction (Green, 2007). In this study, communication mechanisms and organizational supports can help individuals understand the net benefits to both the individual and the organization. Employers can provide an organizational structure that supports behavior to maximize these net benefits.

According to John Scott (Scott, 2000), "approval is the most fundamental goal (in social interaction). Approval is a 'generalized reinforcer' that can reinforce a wide variety of specialized activities." Homans saw approval as equal to money and both can reinforce behavior (Scott, 2000). Money can drive behavior in workplace wellness and some simple examples include penalties from insurers for holding a certified tobacco user status. Additionally, organizations are offering financial rewards for individuals that interact with a health coach, use a personal fitness device, or engage in some forms of physical activities.

As this book unfolds, look for ways that employers can nudge employees toward healthier behaviors; and ways employers do not nudge.

3. THEMES IN WORKPLACE WELLNESS

THEME #1: THE ROLE OF TOP-DOWN SUPPORT

Organizational supports can be described as Human Resource and Leadership related mechanisms that provide assessments, health education, strategic incentives, dedicated labor, funding, and health promotion activities that are developed to improve employee health.

Organizational support and structure from the top-down is critical in the success of wellness programs. According to the literature, over 60% of Americans are present in the workplace. If organizations can be a source of health education and practices, worksites can surpass any other venue for addressing illness before it occurs. The CDC HSC awards points for organizational leaders to encourage their workforce throughout all levels of leadership. Indicators of a strong commitment include a health promotion committee, a paid health promotion coordinator, or a champion who is a strong advocate of the program.

The health risk assessment is a very popular tool in workplace wellness programs in the United States. These assessments are best coordinated by leaders in the organization and the results can be used to develop other wellness program. According to a study of wellness programs conducted by the school of Public Health at Harvard University, 80% of companies with wellness programs use the health risk assessment as the initial requirement in their wellness programs. (Baicker et al., 2010) Participation "is almost always voluntary" and selection bias can be a major problem in these types of programs, because the rest of the programs for all of the employees follow this initial information. (Baicker et al., 2010) If employees are conducting wellness programs on their own, without top-down involvement, the programs are not guided by the results of health risk assessments.

THEME #2: THE IMPORTANCE OF AN UNDERSTANDING MANAGER

One of the leading causes of employee stress and depression can be burnout and exhaustion.

The future of workplace wellness will require organizational leaders to be more understanding and responsive to the needs of their employees. Recent research has found that employees are skeptical of health practices unless they are sure the practices are in the employees' best interests, not just the financial interests of the company. (Dee W. Edington, 2015) The same authors believe that the successful wellness programs of the future are those that focus on the social and emotional context of a supportive workplace, culture, and environment. (Edington, Schultz, Pitts, & Camilleri, 2016) Historically, financial incentives and participation in wellness programs have been the primary measures of success. However, financial gains for the company or participation by an employee only demonstrate short term results. These metrics do not necessarily look at health markers or behavioral change over time.

In addressing employees' stress and anxiety, innovative leaders need to go beyond stress management and find ways to make employees' day-to-day work less stressful. Employers can address stress reduction part of the culture and climate of the organization by setting guidelines for productive meetings, fostering connections between employees, celebrating successes on a regular basis, allowing flexible schedules, and teaching employees how to use technology in less stressful ways, and involving supervisors in managing employees' stress through regularly reviews. (Dee W. Edington, 2015)

A leading cause of this feeling in employees is the 24/7 expectations that accompany the rise of the global company. (Dee W. Edington, 2015) "The human body's stress response system is designed to respond to and resolve acute stressors; the chronic levels of stress experienced by many adults today take an incredible toll on their physical and emotional health in a variety of ways." (Dee W. Edington, 2015) These authors suggest that organizations go further than the CDC HSC suggests and "bar email messages and other forms of communication in the evenings and on weekends." (Dee W. Edington, 2015)

Lastly, employers need to take on the role of a coach or supporter in helping create lasting motivation in their employees. Currently, many wellness efforts have been focused on extrinsic motivators for health and wellness, such as financial incentives, parking spaces, days off, or points that can be exchanged for merchandise. However, the literature suggests that "high financial extrinsic motivators can (eventually) result in lower intrinsic motivation." (Dee W. Edington, 2015) The building of intrinsic motivation can help employees increase self-confidence, self-control, and build connections with others and their environment. People are more likely to practice and adopt behaviors that are promoted by those they feel connected to when they have a trusting relationship. (Dee W. Edington, 2015) An understanding manager is one that helps the employee work toward shared goals of health and wellness, rather than simply providing financial incentives for checking a participation box.

THEME #3: SOCIAL INTERACTION AND PARTICIPATION

The literature suggested that social interaction is helpful for wellness participation. As stated in the previous section, information dissemination and awareness building is a common theme of success in the literature. Effective wellness programs also allow input from employees, or two-way communication when developing clear goals and objectives. (Goetzel et al., 2014)

In the category of Lactation Support, the literature suggested that social interaction in the form of prenatal classes was very important for employee retention. One study in 2004 concluded that there was a 94% return-to-work rate after maternity leave for women participating in an employer sponsored lactation program. (Ortiz, McGilligan, & Kelly, 2004) Social interaction around physical activity may also be a key to participation.

Accessibility to bike paths, footpaths, health clubs, and swimming pools have been found to be associated with increased physical activity, but may be insufficient on their own. (Humpel, Owen, & Leslie, 2002) In successful wellness programs, health professionals focused on previous habits that worked for employees' schedules in developing a physical activity wellness program (King, 1998). This demonstrates that a high-touch and intensive communication practice can increase the likelihood of success. Further, a 'social marketing strategy' that includes community-based surveys, feasibility studies, and focus groups can help to optimize the type, format, location, and date of the program is effective to encourage participation. (King, 1998) Additionally, social programs that encourage companionship and esteem support can be an effective strategy for increasing physical activity in a population. (Cavallo et al., 2012)

In stress management, social interaction was very helpful to participants who were part of a mediation support group. Participants in a workplace study on online support and stress management found that

---

"The percentage of participants who reported practicing meditation at least once per week was greater among those with group support than without group support; 94% versus 54%."
(Allexandre et al., 2016)

Employees also benefit by being included in meetings discussing the decision-making process for issues that impact job stress.

The literature also discusses a three-year, intensive wellness program that helped employees implement lasting habit changes in their lives. This intensive case management example studied employees who enrolled in a "three year program where they had an initial visit and then follow-up appointments every 4-8 weeks for a minimum of eight one-on-one visits in the first year and six visits in the subsequent years." (John et al., 2006) Through education about healthy lifestyles, diet, and exercise, and routine measurements of the biomarkers mentioned above, employees experienced "improved blood pressure and reduced LDL levels." (John et al., 2006)

Social interaction can mean more than inside the organization, as the literature also encourages social interaction throughout the community. The Journal for Environment and Urbanization has a wide-sweeping notion they call the "Spectrum of Prevention," which calls for communities to "strengthen individual knowledge and skills; promoting community education; educating providers and leaders (in all sectors); fostering coalitions and networks; changing organizational practice (within government, health institutions and workplaces, among others); and influencing policy and legislation." (Chehimi, Cohen, & Valdovinos, 2011) This is a broad and wide-sweeping vision for leveraging community resources, but it may be that many of these activities are already happening in a community and simply need coordination. (Committee, 2016)

THEME #4: LINKS BETWEEN PREVENTION AND CHRONIC DISEASE

Seven of the categories of the HSC can work together to increase the health of the workforce. Four preventive categories, Physical Activity, Weight Management, Nutrition, and Tobacco Control can help three of the chronic disease-related categories: High Blood Pressure, High Cholesterol, and Diabetes. An article by Goetzel discusses employees that have biometric values which are abnormally high, specifically pertaining to blood pressure, diabetes, obesity, or cholesterol. (Goetzel, 2008) He states that health promotion in the work place can reach this group by focusing on hypertension screenings, smoking cessation, weight loss education, and/or helping employees overcome financial barriers to healthier choices, such as obtaining medicine to control their biometric values. Abbot and Byrd state that weight loss education can be extremely important because nutrition habits in the United States are well below the Department of Health and Human Services and other widely recognized standards. (Abbot and Byrd, 2007).

Although it is difficult to know where to start, an article by Thorpe suggests that managers may find success in focusing on obesity, as

"Health spending is reportedly 36% higher in obese adults under the age of sixty-five than in normal weight adults." (Thorpe et al., 2004)

He also states that most of this higher spending is due to "treatments for diabetes, hyperlipidemia, and heart disease." (Thorpe et al., 2004)

Nutrition is another category that can help reduce the effects of chronic diseases in the workforce. Mhurchu suggests that employers that provide healthy food in vending machines or cafeterias have been experienced positive effects on CVD risk factors. (Mhurchu, Aston, & Jebb, 2010) Employers are encouraged by the HSC to create a formal policy to make "vegetables, fruits, 100% fruit juices, whole-grain items and trans fat free – low sodium snacks available in vending machines." (CDC, 2014) Company policies can also make healthier foods available during meetings or employee "pitch ins".

Physical activity can help employees reduce the amount of chronic disease in the workplace. A study by the Centers for Disease Control, the Brownson School of Public Health in St. Louis, and others, states that physical activity has many health benefits, "including reduced risk of cardiovascular disease, ischemic stroke, non-insulin-dependent (type 2) diabetes, colon cancers, osteoporosis, depression, and fall-related injuries.(Kahn, Ramsey, Brownson, et al, 2002). The article continues by stating that "despite the benefits of regular physical activity, only 25% of adults in the United States report engaging in the recommended amounts of physical activity." (Kahn et al., 2002)

Weight management efforts can help the financial aspects of organizations' wellness plans, as obese adults incur medical expenses that are 36% to 37.4% higher than those of normal weight adults, due to more office visits, hospital care, and prescription drugs. (Boardley & Pobocik, 2009) Obesity can affect both the quality and length of life and an obese person can have an 8% to 22% reduction in length of life. (MacDonald & Westover, 2011) The weight management efforts rewarded by the CDC HSC often have goals of achieving positive changes in employees' body mass, blood pressure, cholesterol, triglycerides, and glucose levels. (Hyatt Neville, Merrill, & Kumpfer, 2011) Improvements in these levels can positively influence health care costs, productivity, long-term health, job satisfaction, absenteeism, long-term health and a sense of community. (Merrill, Aldana, Garrett, & Ross, 2011)

The organizations in the study offer only a few programs to address chronic conditions related to high blood pressure, high cholesterol, and diabetes. These organizations conduct health screening with a nurse during the on-boarding process and offer ongoing health screenings for all employees. One interviewee shared that they address high blood pressure in the way it relates to stress management. This same organization is affiliated with a medical school, a hospital network, and primary care physicians. Yet, they did not score higher than the average organizations in the validation study.

The interviewees in middle-scoring category did not have knowledge of strong programs. One manufacturer provides a blood pressure testing machine with literature on how to test and interpret one's blood pressure, which enables employees to monitor their own blood pressure and earns points on the CDC HSC. Even so, diabetes, high blood pressure, and high cholesterol, were low scoring categories for them. The low-scoring respondents did not have much knowledge or elaboration on programs to reduce the presence of chronic diseases in their organizations.

THEME #5: CREATE ROUTINE SYSTEMS TO MONITOR HEALTH

Like fast, slow, and carpool lanes on a highway, employers need to offer an approach that provides different wellness programs for different segments of the population. The three segments of the population mentioned by some authors are generally healthy populations, those at high risk for disease, and those with an existing condition that need help managing their diseases or even reversing the effects and cost.

In order to reach all of these populations, a targeted and inclusive overall program is needed. The first types of programs focus on primary prevention efforts and focus on generally healthy populations. These programs can also help workers who do not currently focus on their health, but can prevent diseases if they participate in the program (Goetzel & Ozminkowski, 2008).

The second type of wellness programs can promote health to a second group of individuals that are a high risk for poor health. These individuals are at risk for poor health because they may smoke, work sedentary jobs, drink alcohol excessively, practice unsafe sex, or experience high levels of stress. Encouraging this group to participate in regular physical activity can be extremely important to worksite health.

The third group of health promotion activities that Goetzel identifies is considered disease management for the segment of the population with an existing condition. These programs are directed at individuals with existing ailments, such as "asthma, diabetes, cardiovascular disease, cancers, musculoskeletal disorders, and depression." (Goetzel, 2008) The aim of these types of interventions is to slow down the disease or improve the condition through better adherence to their clinical protocols.

In the area of emergency response, one article found that without a routine checkup of their emergency plans, many organizations' plans would not work in the event they were needed. The authors found that almost all had "written emergency plans, but only 50% posted their plans and only 27% performed the recommended quarterly emergency drills." (Herbert et al., 2007) For instance, workplaces should have an emergency response plan, a team in place, and prior training on CPR and AED usage. In the above study, 73% had an AED, but only 6% reported using it in an emergency. (Herbert et al., 2007)

THEME #6: LEVERAGING THE KNOWLEDGE OF EXPERTS

Leveraging the support of a large corporate office or an industry association can make a difference in an organization's CDC HSC score. The use of proven wellness strategies from professional resources that were integrated into a culture helped organizations achieve a higher score. Borrowing expertise worked better than a mix of activities based on preferences or feelings from individuals that worked in human resources.

The highest-scoring organization in the pilot study contracted with local doctors to create a health assessment based on blood work.

The blood work became their "guiding principle" to know the health an individual or a group of employees. This organization also uses a nation–wide third party group called Live Well that provides them with best practices. Live Well can then provide them with a rating of their wellness programs, based on a five-star rating system. The leaders in this organization also mentioned multiple trips around the country to study the best health practices at other organizations.

An industrial manufacturer in the study uses a program from US Wellness to provide aggregate information on the health of their employees based on their online portal information. They also participate in information sharing meetings in the community and they feel that "based on the fact that we've gone to those meetings with American Heart Association, health and wellness is becoming more and more important in organizations. I think we're kind of ahead of the curve based on what we've seen." This organization also states that as an organization with 125 employees, it is hard for them to offer the same programs as a company with 12,000 employees that also attend their American Heart Association roundtable.

This industrial manufacturer is fairly small at 125 employees, but they leverage the resources of their large corporate office. The corporate office requires an on-site garden and gym and provides the resources for each location to implement these at their site. The corporate office also has templates for many wellness educational programs and competitions. Finally, they leverage resources in the community by hosting a health and wellness fair with local wellness vendors and organizations. The wellness fair was a common theme amongst the high-scoring organizations in the pilot study.

A social services organization works through their insurance provider, United Healthcare, to utilize a program called Simply Engage. This program is described as a "program that has employees designate different check marks with respect to measures that maintain health and wellness. They can then earn various gift cards, with the biggest one up to a $25 dollars monthly premium reduction." The HR Coordinator states that the Simply Engage program "is what helps me to be able to get people to participate in the weight loss challenge and to participate in the biometrics. Biometrics can get you up to $75 dollar gift card or something like that. There are certain things that you have to do to get to each level. If those incentives weren't in there, I'm not sure how much buy-in we would get from everyone." Additionally, they leverage the YMCA during the month of January, because the monthly membership fees are reduced at the first of the year. Anyone can take advantage of the YMCA's cheaper rate, but this organization promotes the discounted fees and provides further incentives for employees that participate.

The two lower-scoring organizations in the pilot study demonstrate the results when an organization does not take advantage of resources that are available to them. One organization in the pilot study has nineteen local employees, but is part of an organization with over five thousand employees.

Because their corporate office is three hours away, they do not take advantage of the world-class (and often free) services provided there.

According to their interviewee, this caused their score to be below average, 99 out of a possible 264. They could have increased their score by leveraging the communication materials sent from their corporate office.

For instance, points are awarded for newsletters, videos, brochures, and webinars on the topics of the CDC HSC. These things are all available, but at the local level, they do not act as a conduit of this information.

The other lower-scoring organization in the pilot study is a world-wide organization in their niche. They are in twelve countries and forty-six states and their local office has 66 employees. Their local office does not pass or share resources from their global network, even though those resources do exist. This reduces their score and the overall health of the employees.

THEME #7: OFFER A VARIETY OF WELLNESS PROGRAMS IN EACH CATEGORY

A variety of wellness programs helps meet employees at their level of interest. For instance, a wellness competition can be self-reporting or managed by the organization. A wellness competition can involve a year-long walking event where employees try to "Walk across the Midwest" or America. A weight loss competition, eating veggies for a number of times each week, engaging in wellness education, attending the gym a certain number of times, or walking a "baby-k," one-kilometer track around the property are examples of programs offered.

Likewise, communication is most effective when it is done in different mediums. As long as the information is consistent, the following methods can be effective: brochures, online literature, person-to-person in group meetings or individually, YouTube or intranet videos, the organization's bulletin boards, or third party providers. The highest-scoring organization in the pilot study used one-on-one coaching, 360-degree feedback, employee blood work, the cost of Emergency Department visits, and the level of participation to determine the success of their wellness efforts.

In the physical movement category, organizations in this study also demonstrate a variety of exercise initiatives to appeal to a broad range of employees. The movement practices included standing, walking, running groups, yoga, weight-lifting, climbing stairs, and country line dancing. The organizations had a basketball goal, a ping pong table, cornhole boards, and a walking track on site. With each of these physical structure supports, they have programs to engage employees. For instance, there are free throw contests and walking contests; even if these competitions are employees competing with their previous scores.

A unique way of meeting employees where they are was demonstrated in the work day schedules. One organization has created a "school day program." This program allows "working mothers or dads that have kids in school to come in to work from 9:00 am to 2:00 pm, Monday through Friday, and then be off so they don't have to pay for childcare." This program allows employees to be home with the kids when they're not in school, such as a snow day or if a child is sick. The industrial manufacturer in the pilot study has different methods of providing flexible time for their employees. They currently have "about seven or eight or more different schedules, so if you wanted to come in from 7:30 am to 4:00 pm, that was probably doable."

The organization in the technical services industry has less formal methods for helping their employees with flexible schedules. For instance, if an employee does a lot of work in a particular day, but does not finish or make great progress on their current project, they can still leave after a full day's work. The Senior Recruiter explained that their managers "will tell you, listen, you had a good day, go home. It's okay. Relax a little bit. My manager (said), that as long as you make the most of your day from 8 to 5, if you need to leave at 5 to go to your yoga class, go ahead and do it." Although this is not a formal policy, it does demonstrate flexibility with employee's schedules.

THEME #8: SAFETY AS A TREND

If other aspects of health and wellness can be taken as seriously as safety, it will change the health landscape of the entire nation.

Safety was trend in these organizations, as many scored high on safety, even if they did not particularly focus on other aspects of health and wellness. The organizations in the highest scoring category emphasized occupational health and safety as integral to their worksite wellness activities. The 1500-employee automobile supplier stated that emergency response teams (ERT's) are on staff at every facility, every day. They are trained regularly in CPR and with defibrillators. Similarly, the educational services industry requires all employees to engage in trainings on occupational health and safety annually. The table below shows the scores of companies in this study, compared to the CDC study, for the category of occupational health and safety.

The organizations in the highest scoring category emphasized occupational health and safety as integral to their worksite wellness activities. They are trained regularly in CPR and with defibrillators and many required all employees to engage in trainings on occupational health and safety annually. Interviewees shared that the nature of their business requires them to adhere to a high level of occupational health and safety regulations. These companies are not only held to OSHA regulations, but in some cases also by the Food and Drug Administration regulations, and hazard materials regulations.

Even organizations that scored in the middle of this study take workplace safety very seriously at all levels of their organization. Many interviewees stated that safety is extremely relevant in the immediate workplace and that "the job is dangerous for the majority of our employees." Some organizations feel that occupational health and safety is the number one goal. Nearly all organizations encourage the reporting of injuries and near misses. Multiple organizations have safety fairs periodically where vendors come into their facility and set up booths.

An interviewee from an electrical company emphasized that occupational health and safety is a major part of their work on a day-to-day basis. He stated that:

"Being in the construction industry, OSHA is big, and big for company insurance. Emergency response is probably the only unpreventable incident on a job site that somebody could do something about."

"Some of the CPR training is required by law or required by insurance. If somebody has an electric shock, you need to have someone trained in CPR because proper first aid and CPR could be the difference of life and death." If other aspects of health and wellness can be taken as seriously as safety, it will change the health landscape of the entire nation.

THEME #9: SMOKING AND TOBACCO CONTROL

Smoking was a theme that most organizations struggled with, even high-scoring organizations. The use of tobacco can be extremely detrimental to employee health and wellness as it is an indicator for a variety of chronic diseases. The CDC HSC devotes an entire section to tobacco control in the organizational culture and wellness program. Organizations can demonstrate tobacco control by having written and posted policies that ban tobacco use on company property through multiple channels of communication. Organizations can take active steps to encourage employees to stop using tobacco. These types of supports include stop-smoking telephone lines, subsidizing the cost of tobacco cessation medications and nicotine replacement products, and cessation counseling. The table below shows that twelve of the organizations in the study were below the CDC study average. The interviews explained that tobacco usage was still a problem, even in organizations that scored well in the tobacco control category.

In the highest-scoring category, companies shared that they have designated smoking areas on the property, employees can only smoke in their car, and that visiting contractors who are smoking needed to be coached on tobacco policies. Another organization had on-site police and security with extra time, and they took up the cause of tobacco cessation by passing out samples of nicotine gum.

Some organizations mandate an entirely tobacco free campus, while others have designated tobacco areas. Many employers stated that they incentivize employees to not smoke by providing health points for being tobacco free for a period of time. In some cases, organizations had tobacco policies, but these were mostly due to productivity or safety due to flammable materials.

One interviewee stated that the security force passed out cessation gum and offered counseling or cessation classes for full-time employees.

Another organization is a manufacturer with flammable materials, so tobacco control is a safety issue, as well as a health issue. Most organizations have insurance that pays for cessation or provides discounts for being a certified non-smoker. Organizations without a tobacco free campus still follow city, county, and state laws for smoking, such as an employee cannot smoke within so many feet of the door.

Many of the more blue-collar employers have cultures where most of the people at the organization smoke, even when there are serious health care incentives for being a non-tobacco user. One interviewee did not feel that tobacco control was an important issue because one colleague had lung cancer, but it did not slow down tobacco use. Another organization had strong evidence of tobacco use and the interviewee felt that employees would really be upset if the company suggested that they quit smoking. Several of these organizations dealt with smoking employees by providing a smokers shack or requiring employees to smoke in their cars. One could wonder about the health effects of smoking in an enclosed shack or enclosed car in bad weather.

THEME #10: EMPLOYING CHOICE ARCHITECTURE

Choice Architecture, described by the Nudge Theory, was a theme in the successful organizations of this study. Organizations in this study have wellness programs that gently encouraged employers to engage in healthy behavior. The Nudge Theory was used to determine whether employers guide employees to healthier behavior using 'choice architecture'. Choice architecture is a conscious or unconscious practice of setting up organizational structures to guide the population to behave in certain ways.

Organizations with higher scores in the study seemed to nudge employees into health screenings during orientation or on a regular basis.

Participation in health screenings result in cheaper health insurance, financial incentives, or even a substantial contribution to the employee's health savings account.

The post-health-screening actions vary from optional feedback, to moderate feedback, to intensive one-on-one coaching for an extended period of time. The intensive coaching was described by one participant as "every quarter a nurse comes in and checks everybody that wants it, and then if you need something you contact her by emailing her. Then she will come in the next day. That way it's not permanent that you have to go to her, you can also use your own doctor or get someone else." This is a nudge because it is readily available, but it is not mandatory that you see the company's nurse.

Another example of encouraging healthy choices was that that if employees participate in a Weight Watchers program for twelve weeks, they get it for twelve weeks for free. The interviewee further elaborated that "if you lose so much weight, you get a Fitbit." Other incentives include free flu shots, free gym memberships for a facility that is within walking distance of their campus, and free time around lunch to attend the gym.

Other organizations used a points system to track doctor visits, gym usage, and wellness competitions. Employees can then redeem their points for merchandise. Uniquely, one organization, provided employees a financial bonus for using all their vacation time. It can even be argued that inexpensive health insurance and other insurance benefits can nudge employees to healthy behavior. For instance, a $40 copay and very cheap insurance might allow people to see a health care provider, when they might not.

The CDC HSC considers flexible attitudes and flexible schedules a component of healthy environments. High-scoring organizations in this study were very flexible with time off for illness and pursuing school. Two organizations in the highest-scoring category encourage community outreach through "volunteer time off" for employees to participate in community events. These programs are nudges because the organization does not mandate the type of community outreach, but they do provide time off and flexibility through supervisors.

Some employers may not promote healthy activities, but they do not discourage them either. Allowing the conditions for healthy activities can be considered a nudge as well. One employee stated that walks and exercise at his company are employee driven amongst friends. Another interviewee stated that employees are encouraged to take a walk during any time of the work day. Leaders even encourage the entire office to go out and take a walk on the nearby street. One employer in the study made every employee part of a pair in case the employees wanted to take a walk, talk about work, attend yoga, or another social or healthy activity. Again, this was encouraged, but not required.

Removing obstacles can allow healthy actions to naturally take place, rather than just incentivizing employees to participate. These methods of encouraging employees are examples of Nudge Theory and Choice Architecture that have been previously discussed. For instance, the highest scoring organization found that employees were not using their on-site clinic because they did not want to use personal or vacation time to go to the clinic.

"The organization gave every employee six hours of free time to use for visiting a clinic or primary care facility."

They are not required to go to the on-site clinic, but the company removed a common barrier to encourage employees to use the clinic.

Another organization encourages intramural activities by providing the entry fees and uniforms for their employees. These activities are not on company time, but the managers allow employees to leave on time to make it to intramural games and practice.

All of the organizations in the pilot study have access to an employee-assistance program, but not all of the organizations promote their EAP program. By educating and allowing employees to access to these resources, the employees that want this kind of help will naturally take advantage of resources for tobacco cessation, depression, work-related stress, financial counseling, and other personal issues. One organization stated that tobacco cessation counseling can happen through their Employee Assistance Program (EAP) and they offer a $500 reimbursement program for cessation. Their HR Manager stated that, "I've talked to several people about (quitting) but we also have it as part of our EAP program. We have all the US Wellness programs and starting this year, the US Wellness tobacco cessation program requires employees to take four-week cessation online course." This program can be completed at work if necessary.

Another example of allowing healthy habits to naturally happen occurs in the area of nutrition. Several of the organizations offer free food that is healthy, but employees have to pay for unhealthy food. One organization placed healthy snacks near their workout room so employees will take advantage of this food when they are thinking in a health conscious way and hungry after working out. Further, employers allow employees to bring in food from their gardens to share with other employees. The organizations could ban this because it is outside food, but they provide a space and clean up after the employees bring in their food.

PART 2: THE FIRST DIMENSION OF WORKPLACE WELLNESS: ORGANIZATIONAL SUPPORTS

4. ORGANIZATIONAL CULTURE

"Health risk assessments can uncover "latent disease" and allow interventions in the early stages of disease, where they are easier and cheaper to treat."

The CDC HSC encourages employers to support their workforce in very broad, wide-reaching ways at the organizational and/or upper management level. The structure and policies of the organization can tell a lot about their commitment to health and wellness. Indicators of a strong commitment include a health promotion committee, a paid health promotion coordinator, or a champion who is a strong advocate of the program. An annual health promotion budget, organizational objectives, and a mission statement that includes employee wellness programs are all indicators of a strong commitment at the highest levels of the organization. Many organizations use a health risk assessment as the initial intervention and a necessary step for individuals to enter a wellness program.

The organizations in the pilot study have a range of wellness cultures that demonstrate the embedded values and norms of their organizations. The automobile manufacturer, who scored nearly perfect on the CDC HSC has shared many world class practices from their organization. At the same time, they have a culture that does embrace health and wellness, even in spite of all the resources and education the company provides. They say

"You'll see a guy get the Big AZ Burger, go get two Diet Mountain Dews, sit down and hammer them down then go out and smoke a cigarette."

(The Big AZ Burger is a third party vendor that sells hamburgers on the company's property.) Further studies could investigate this specific employer, their culture, and how well they are doing in spite of the local feelings toward smoking and nutrition.

An industrial manufacturer used a time of transition to implement wellness programs into the culture. The organization launched these programs with employees that were volunteering and soliciting the help of other volunteers who were not being paid for the extra work they did on wellness initiatives. During this time of transition, they had members of the HR department implement and manage wellness programs in addition to the other parts of their position. According to their Health Program Coordinator, "I would say honestly, it's because we were in a transition. Before the HR Manager came, we were in that transition with our HR. We had started it when (the previous HR Manager) was here and then we continued the programs and then with the US Wellness resources from corporate, it was a continuous thing."

Their Health Program Champion, continued by saying:

"We didn't have an HR program before (the HR Manager) came and so then, me and another associate out on the floor were volunteered."

We were told to keep the wellness committee going because it's such a big thing within the company, you can't let it go. So we were supposed to just be in charge until we hired someone. Well then, it took a while to get somebody on. Then we continued and the people that were before us in HR had started the process of adding to it and building things with our committee here because the local committees at each plant get to choose how and what they do to a certain extent."

An organization in the social services industry suggested that they have an understanding attitude when it comes to employee injuries or safety-related mistakes. The organization has a policy of retraining individuals from the ground up, in lieu of punishment and reprimands. Their HR Coordinator believes that this aspect of their culture encourages employees to report minor injuries and mistakes, rather than covering the mistakes up. According to the HR Coordinator, when a mistake is made, instead of giving a punishment, "the employee needs to retake that program. Whether it's A and B or A or B. It's not necessarily just 'you did wrong. Reprimand. Reprimand.' But okay, this something happened. Let's get you retrained so that we cannot have that happen again."

An organization from the technical services industry stated that their culture does not have anything official relating to wellness. They have some activities that encourage wellness, such as intramural teams and walking the stairs, but their culture does not hold wellness as a major priority. According to their senior recruiter, wellness is not a priority because the company is too busy. In this interviewee's words, the culture of wellness "is just nothing official really, because, to be honest, it's not that it's not a priority but it's just not a huge stress.

"We're not an insurance company, we're not a healthcare company. We're a business...we're too busy, we've got too much other stuff to do."

The organizations in the second phase of the study have a range of wellness cultures that demonstrate their embedded values and norms. Two organizations in the highest-scoring category encourage community outreach. These companies provide employees VTO or "volunteer time off" for employees to participate in community events. An automobile supplier has a program called EEEC, which stands for Every Employee Every Community. This program allows the employee to choose a project of their choice. According to one of their engineers, the company "doesn't say we'll help out, Blessings in a Backpack, or we'll help out this or that group. They'll allow me four hours a month that they pay me and I can just leave work and still be on company time technically. I could go work for Habitat for Humanity or the Animal Shelter, or wherever I choose to."

A twenty-five employee manufacturing organization in the highest-scoring group also allows VTO for its employees. According to their quality engineer, "we have VTO. Volunteer time off, and that's why I'm always volunteering at Purdue. My boss loves it. They love it when we participate in outside community projects."

An engineer at the automobile supplier feels that there is a culture of caring and concern for all of the employees. In his words, "there are a lot of large companies that people feel like (they) just show up and push the button. They feel as though there are a million people that want to take my spot and I'm expendable." They interviewee feels that his company "doesn't look at their people like they're expendable and there's a lot of long-term employees there. And I think it's because of the safety stuff, and the promoting of wellness." This statement could be explored in further research to see if these organizations experience less employee turnover than companies that do not invest in these programs.

This individual shared a story about the culture and their attitude toward helping employees with their drug or alcohol addiction. The interviewee has ten years of sobriety and another employee learned of the interviewee's sobriety and shared his experience at work. The employee spent three to four weeks in addiction treatment, paid for by the company.

> *"The employee's life was falling apart, 'alcohol was wrecking him' and the company ensured that he had the resources he needed to return to a healthy state of mind and body."*

The employee of the aforementioned 25-employee organization also feels like he matters to the organization, in terms of being an asset to the company and feeling like they are part of a family. He elaborated on this point by sharing that "my boss treats us like a giant family. Twice a month, we have a company picnic where everybody goes out with their families.

The whole HR department helps promote these ideas that plan and implement these health programs."

He further explained that the family feeling even expands beyond employees to their actual families. For instance, an employee can add their wife, husband, or child, if they have an illness. The interviewee shared that "employees can bring in family members in and speak to the nurse without a fee. For instance, one of the guys I work with, his wife is pregnant and she's got high blood pressure, because they're worried about her with the baby. So they brought her in, and they actually gave her prescriptions for medication. She's not one of the employees; she's just one of the employee's wives." In another example, one of the employees' children is diabetic and they help the family.

This organization also has visible goals for employee health on display in the break room. Since their company deals with chemistry, the goals are displayed with a big beaker that sits on the wall. The employee shared that "one of the guys is an artist. So he draws them up, and then we have goals reviews each week. Every time we fill a goal, we shade it in to a certain point. Then we get to a certain point and the company hosts a more fancy lunch during one of our lunch and learns. So the company pays more for lunch." The interviewee feels that if the company was bigger, they probably wouldn't have all the benefits they have. Further research might investigate the benefits of large companies versus the benefits of small companies, who each had the same or similar CDC HSC scores.

The organization in the electronics manufacturing industry has several examples of the way culture helps shape the health and wellness activities of a workforce. According to their engineer, the company pays "very big premiums" each year to bring out of pocket health care costs down for the employees. They also provide a very generous vacation and free-time program. According to the employee that has worked there for eight years, "in about a year, I'll get another week of vacation. So, I'll get three weeks of vacation a year. Then you get a week of personal time on top of that."

This organization also has a marked interest in physical activity. They were mentioned earlier in the study as the organization where the supervisors play basketball with their employees on a weekly basis. The engineer stated that:

> *"Physical activity would definitely be the highest category because people here are pretty active ... a lot of people take walks, they do CrossFit, people play basketball."*

They're aware that they can move about. There are a lot of people here that are pretty healthy. People do well here (financially) so they can afford to have these more active lifestyles. Even so, there are a few people that choose to remain sedentary. One employee used to run a freaking workout store out of his desk!" The organization helped their employees be active by building a shower in the building now, right by the break room.

The organizations in the study have a range of wellness cultures that demonstrate the embedded values and norms of their organizations. The medium-scoring group shared a long list of health and wellness themes in the culture of their organizations. For instance, the leadership team in the utilities industry took up donations to pay the above-insurance expenses for a sick employee. According to their project engineer, an employee had lung cancer, and had a quarter of his lung removed. "The leadership team took up donations to pay for what his health insurance wouldn't pay. The employees had all of his vacation days used up and everybody donated their days. They actually raised enough money and vacation days to keep him off work for eight months." This type of support in the culture demonstrates that the organization really cares about their employees.

Another organization's culture promotes their open enrollment in smaller groups. For instance, a supervisor will communicate the deadlines and benefits of enrolling to a group of five to ten people. According to their supervisor,

> *"The health messages are delivered in smaller settings of one supervisor speaking to five to ten people, so we know those people pretty intimately."*

He further elaborated that when the company was bigger, they had a health promotion committee, but some of these activities have decreased, "just for the fact that we've gone from a place that had 130 employees down to 70 employees." Although the smaller employee number has decreased their resources, it has allowed them to communicate more intimately.

A 3-D Design organization, with 30 employees, had a strong culture that emphasized physical activity and participating in exercise movements in groups. The 3-D designer stated that "we were encouraged to take a walk during any time of the work day. We call it coffee walk. Sometimes the entire office would go out and take a walk on the nearby street. Sometimes, we walk as comrades, too, so we would pair up every month with someone else, and then we would do different activities. With our comrade, we might take a walk, talk about work or different stuff related to personal lives or something like that." The company also paid for a gym membership at the YMCA.

The 3-D Design organization also celebrated role models and health-related successes as part of their organizational culture. The interviewee described their culture by saying "everything was just open and public all the time. So for example, when I did CrossFit, they would always ask about it, and then talk about different things that all of us are doing." The employees in the office also play basketball together several times a week. According to the designer, "there are a lot of spontaneous things that the company does also. There are times a bunch of us take bike rides around the park for half a day. Also, we would get together and run in the morning around the park and come back and shower at work. We have a shower and everything provided for us."

From their employee's viewpoint, this organization mainly focused on efficiency and if the job was done. If employees wanted to take long walks, work from home, or play basketball during the work day, it was ok as long as the work was done. The interviewee described it by saying that "if employees can be productive certain numbers of hours and get to work even to work from home, that was a win-win situation for the company. The enjoyment level of employees was also important and we had such an open environment culture, which everyone just absolutely loved. For the most part, for me, it never felt like I was going to work" This contrasts with the largest organization in the study whose:

"Company culture does not seem to care about employee well-being and "just cares about the work getting done."

The organization in the transportation and automation industry displayed a culture of health and wellness that helped them score above average in this study. A lot of their culture was employee-ran, rather than being mandated or officially supported by the corporation. Their engineer stated that "we use to, as a group, go to the gym. Unfortunately, the gym closed but there was a group of us that religiously went to the gym at lunch. You can't say it was promoted by the job because it was just all of us going but at the same time it was (work-related) because we were all there. We were all working there and we were all encouraging each other so it was like a culture within our little cubicle section." Perhaps the employees would have continued this ritual if the employer provided a gym on-site. Further research could look into the participation rates of on-site company gyms.

Although this organization does not exactly support a lot of health initiatives, it seemed as though they did not prohibit healthy activities. Further, the company would help employees with health-related issues when they did ask for help. The interviewee from this organization stated that "I've had positive experiences in that if I express a need for something, they'll provide it, but at the same time I don't see a lot of promotion from them. There's a guy that keeps saying 'Hey man, that's a great standing desk. How would I get one?' I told him a few times and he said 'Well, I did that, but they didn't follow suit.' I was just thinking, it was so easy for me I don't know how it's so hard for him. It leads me to believe that not everybody has the same positive outlook." This raises an interesting point because a company's proactive stance in promoting health initiatives can make all the difference to employees who are not proactive. Further research could investigate the success of company's programs based on the amount of promotion they include with their initiatives.

The last comment this interviewee shared about his organization's culture related to community involvement. This aspect of social wellness was employee-ran, like their gym example from above.

"We do assorted community involvement projects like gathering toys for children during Christmas and we conduct winter coat drives."

An electrician supervisor from the construction industry felt that the entire culture of the construction industry made it difficult to implement health and wellness programs. In the interview, he stated that:

41

"My gut tells me it's an alpha male dominated industry, and the employees say 'you're not going to tell me how to live my life' or 'I don't know if that's right.'

I don't know. Sometimes men don't ask for help with these things, maybe." This employee and another in the lowest-scoring category, felt that, in the construction industry, employees are always moving. Therefore, even if they are not healthy by the numbers, but they can still move around, their poor health does not have a visible effect on job performance.

The electrician supervisor further explained how the culture in the construction industry affected health and wellness. He felt that "there's nobody that's educated on health and wellness. The company's not going to go do that.... also, it has to do with how wide spread people are. It's not like everybody works at one location. They don't' have a place where they can funnel everyone, tell them 'here we're bringing this program in.' If we're bringing somebody in, the rest of the company is still out there." Further research could explore organizations that excel in health and wellness with a widespread workforce to see if the spread out nature is a true reason for having very little health programming.

Another organization in the technical services industry explained the same challenges in promoting health and wellness with a workforce that travels out from a home office. The interviewee from this organization stated that the leadership must focus on employee health intensively while the workforce is in the corporate office because they will be on the road for months. According to their systems engineer, "our high scoring areas (in the HSC) go directly with keeping employees safe. While we're gone, traveling on the road, they don't want you to get the flu or anything like that on the road so they handle things like that. Additionally, if you have a heart attack, they don't want you to die while you're on the road, so they want to have something in place to where that doesn't happen. I think they've had an episode like that happen before, and that may play a major part in (current policies)."

This employee further stated that the company has decreased the focus on health as they have gotten larger. In the interviewee's words, "to reduce turnover, they have been focusing on getting people to stay and getting more people in the workforce. They're growing more than they even have enough people to support." It also sounds like any focus on health, wellness, and safety leans heavily toward safety because the individuals over these areas are formally housed in the safety department. The interviewee continued, "The people who actually have anything to do with the health and safety are really in safety and they'll talk to you about it. They act like they want you to be as safe as can be."

The last organization in the middle-scoring category seemed to have a culture of health and safety that is directly tied to financial costs of poor health and safety. This organization leads stretching programs at the beginning of every shift and after lunch. According to their employee,

---

"As far as workplace wellness goes, there wasn't really a lot of stuff that was done in your day-to-day work. They had medical staff on site in case somebody dropped from being lightheaded or there was a physical injury."

He continued that "the wellness programs are geared toward functionality and productivity."

Similar to the previous organization that focused on safety over health and wellness, this retail/wholesale trade company houses their health and wellness initiatives in the safety function of their organization. According to the interviewee, "they stressed the 5S methodology. 5S is sort, set in order, shine, standardize, and sustain." In this philosophy, safety is often seen as the sixth 'S', one that is included in the other five S activities and in everything employees do. The interviewee shared that "they wanted to stress that you were going to be safe, number one, and then have fun second, and then productivity. But they didn't live by it." The employee seemed to feel that productivity was the reason for the safety and that fun was not emphasized much at all.

The six companies in the lowest-scoring category of this study discussed a number of themes in their culture relating to wellness. Perhaps these themes shed light on cultures that do not necessarily support health and wellness in the eyes of their employees. For instance, an interviewee from an automobile supplier in this category shared that employees "on the floor" would either have to take paid time off or vacation time to go to the doctor. Of course, this contrasts with the higher scoring companies in the study that allow time off to visit the doctor or even to volunteer.

Additionally, the employee felt that their culture does not support health and wellness because they are having enough trouble simple satisfying their customers' needs in the moment. In the interviewee's words, "they are not a structured company." The reason is because they started up two years ago, they're having, I would say, system failures with producing product. So, a lot of it is crunch time. They're doing a lot of overworking, working seven days a week for all three shifts. When they get structure could they possibly focus more on this but their attention is elsewhere right now."

Another manufacturer in the study felt that their company's culture leads to healthy behavior in the areas of alcohol and tobacco. For instance, the interviewee stated that the company is very 'straight edge' when it comes to alcohol and tobacco and they are not tolerated. He further stated that:

"I think tobacco control is mainly because I would say the lifestyle of the owners influence that a lot...they're very straight edge when it comes to any alcohol being in the workplace or any tobacco or any kind of substance."

The interviewee also felt that the age of the employees affected the culture and the company's approach to health and wellness. There is not a feeling of needing weight loss or health programs because everyone is so young. He stated that "with everybody being so young, I wonder if there's no need to have a weight loss program and things like that. Further research can study the changes at this company throughout the years when everybody gets older and employees become more diverse in age and how they will adapt to that in health programs.

In spite of the youth of their organization, the employee feels that there is a lot of stress in the employees. He also stated that stress management is one of the areas where they want to improve in order to decrease employee turnover. The interviewee did feel that the company definitely cares for the employees. He felt that if something "was an issue that was very prominent, it was obvious that it was an issue, they would address it."

A small manufacturing firm of 43 employees does not have a strong wellness culture or a lot of resources to promote health and wellness. However, they can help the employees with stress and earn points on the CDC HSC by providing flexible schedules. According to their quality assurance engineer, they have two first shifts, on two different times. The employee felt that this helps individuals with different personal or family situations. In his words, "some people like to come in at 7 and work till 4 and some people like to come in at 5:30 and work till 2. So we have those two going at the same time. And then also, some like work 10's and some don't. For instance, if you get your 40 hours and you can tell them ahead of time, like two weeks ahead of time, that you need to do something, you can work 4 10's and on Friday you can get off and take care of your needs."

A small shop in technical services industry felt that there culture did not support health and wellness through classes, because they are only a seven-person organization. However, their culture is very caring and helpful if employees need flexibility for their health and wellness needs. According to their interviewee,

"One employee was off for several months for open-heart surgery and continued to get paid."

"My uncle, he had open heart surgery, he was off for several months. He still has doctor visits. He has to go to get check-ups and he's paid for his time off to see the doctor."

The interviewee further stated that he felt their small size was an asset in creating a culture of caring about one another. He shared that "probably because we're so small and when you're a small company, you can't afford to lose even one employee. A bigger company, if you lose one person, it ain't no big deal. You don't even really feel the repercussion of it. If you're a small company of seven, you lose one person you feel it. I guess that's probably the reason why safety is a big thing." He also felt that the closeness of a small company creates a family environment. In his words, "basically we are all family. We all just try to help each other out. It means if you're sick or whatever, we try to help you or work with you as best we can."

Another small organization, with only six employees, feels that their size allows them to also have a flexible culture with employees and how they schedule their time. The journeyman electrician stated that:

"We make it easy for people to make up hours.
Whatever they've got to do, or leave for few hours,
and make it up that afternoon or that weekend."

This individual also felt that the nature of their work kept employees somewhat healthy because they are moving around and very physical in their labor. In explaining their health programs and culture, the employee stated that their health programs are not promoted "in an official way, we do have people that work for us that work out, and you can tell they're healthier than your average bear, but not in an official way."

One downside of their culture, according to the interviewee, is that it is not progressive in thinking of health and wellness as priorities. He shared that he feels uneasy about proposing many of the health and wellness initiatives rewarded by the CDC HSC because they would seem very foreign to his colleagues and the initiatives would not be accepted in the culture. In his words, "I don't want to seem like I think I'm superior, but you just deal with a certain class of people in construction. A lot of it is that everybody has a big huge pride and egos and even mentioning some of these programs would hurl insults your way. You know what I mean? It's like a machismo, like 'That shit's gay. Don't even say that.'" Further research could investigate if this is a widely held opinion in this industry, as the interviewee felt and how the opinion differs in other age groups, educational demographics, or geographies.

Similarly, the lowest-scoring organization in our study has a culture that is not very accepting of health and wellness. The interviewee had a story of a period during his employment when he was trying to engage in more physical activity by jogging during his lunch hour. He described how he would be ridiculed for wearing running attire and jogging within sight of the office. He stated that "I would change into my running attire and shoes at lunch and go run around the (office). I remember daily just getting made fun of. That's aggravating when you're trying to do something healthy. I'm not a professional runner but I ran for a two-week stint. I probably went from a 16-17 minute mile to a 10 minute 30 second mile. I was like 'that's pretty good, an improvement.' Then I hurt my knee. I switched to running shoes I bought at a running store and my knee was damaged after a couple days. It started getting worse and worse. I was running about 45 minutes at lunch every day. Well I didn't run the whole time but then the third day my knee was just, I was limping bad. I just never got back into it. It's aggravating. Yeah you're doing something good…trying, and they want to give you a hard time."

USE OF THE HEALTH RISK ASSESSMENT

Determining the current state of the employee's health and wellness gives leaders a baseline of understanding their wellness strengths and weaknesses. This can help leaders to develop a budget, plan activities, and provide a sense of urgency to address any serious problems as soon as possible.

As stated, according to a study of wellness programs conducted by the school of Public Health at Harvard University, 80% of companies with wellness programs use the health risk assessment as the initial requirement in their wellness programs. (Baicker et al., 2010) Participation in health risk assessments "is almost always voluntary" and

---

Selection bias can be a major problem in these types of programs, because the rest of the programs for all of the employees follow this initial information.
(Baicker et al., 2010)

The literature suggests another problem with wellness programs that are based on health risk assessments. Interventions are commonly applied to everyone, regardless of their health status. If employers were able to target wellness programs to employees based on health status and needs, the targeted approach would yield better results. (Dee W. Edington, 2015)

For effective wellness programs, these assessments and appraisals must include focus groups or satisfaction surveys to determine the effectiveness of the programs. Assessments cannot merely be general employee satisfaction surveys; they need to examine the effectiveness of health promotion programs. Organizations then need to provide individual feedback on health risk appraisals through one-on-one counselling or individualized written reports or letters. Health risk assessments (HRAs) are valuable because they can increase awareness of risk factors, provide guidance for improving one's lifestyle, and ensure those with risk factors are being adequately treated. (Arena et al., 2013). HRAs can uncover "latent disease" and allow interventions in the early stages of disease, where it is easier and cheaper to treat. (Arena et al., 2013)

Wellness programs that provide rewards for completing a participatory health risk assessment are the most common type of wellness program in the United States. (Pomeranz, 2015) The incentives provided by these programs can raise concerns about their voluntary nature and the Americans with Disabilities Act of 1990 states that employers cannot require health-related inquiries and exams. (Pomeranz, 2015). Information gathered from a health risk assessment, such as weight, blood pressure, or blood lipid levels or any other biometric data must be voluntary because it can determine health status, physical activity, or smoking activity. (Mello & Rosenthal, 2008) All of this data must be handled in compliance with HIPPA, the ADA, GINA, and be treated as confidential and separate from personnel records. (EEOC, 2011)

High financial incentives can be discriminatory against lower-wage employees because of the incentive-to-wage ratio.

Another way that wellness incentives can be discriminatory is related to the scale of the financial incentives in relation to the employees' salaries. Edington and Schultz state that high financial incentives can be discriminatory against lower-wage employees because of the incentive-to-wage ratio. (Dee W. Edington, 2015) Edington and Schultz further stated that employees in lower functions in the organizational chart, they cannot really afford to miss the high wellness incentives. An employee in an above average or high earning category may be able to avoid wellness programs because they do not need the money that the incentives produce. In the early days of wellness programs, the incentives began as hats and t-shirts, but current incentives include $50, $100, $300, or even $900 to participate in certain wellness programs.(Dee W. Edington, 2015)
I
An article in the American Journal of Lifestyle Medicine stated that employers need to shift the focus of their wellness programs from best practices to next practices. These authors, Edington and Schultz, feel that

the best practices have focused on screenings, preventative programs, and reduce costs to the company. They describe "next practices" as those that focus on the social and emotional context of a supportive workplace, culture, and environment. (Edington et al., 2016) Recent research has found that employees are skeptical of health practices unless they are sure the practices are in the employees' best interests, not just the financial interests of the company. (Dee W. Edington, 2015)

Further ways that organizations can demonstrate overall support is to provide incentives or competitions to drive behavioral change in employees. Employers can spotlight a role-model employee, assign a health champion, and create an annual budget to demonstrate their support and structural commitment to health and wellness. The CDC HSC provides an example budget that organizations can use to being their wellness initiatives. (CDC, 2014) More in-depth actions to demonstrate organizational support are workplaces promoting their health programs by using a logo, frequent informational messages, and multiple channels of communications. This can include role models that demonstrate the appropriate behavior or success stories that applaud the efforts of employees whose actions align with the company values of health.

To show support, the CDC guides organizations to include individuals of different literacy levels, different cultural backgrounds, and multi-generational issues in the workplace. If health programs reach a population aged 50 and older, the programs can reach a population whom over half indicate they have hypertension and 44% have high cholesterol. (Lind, 2011) Furthermore, 31.2% of workers aged 45-64 have a body mass index over 30 compared with 19.7% of workers ages 18-29, meaning older workers are more likely to be obese. (Luckhaupt, Cohen, Li, & Calvert, 2014) Health issues in older demographics can lead to early retirements, both planned and unplanned. (Benz, 2013) Arthritis, poor mobility, and symptomatic depression can also be a significant source of early retirement for older workers. (Caban-Martinez et al., 2011) Failing to reach this segment of the workforce can leave significant opportunities unaddressed.

Other ways to receive points in this section is to conduct ongoing evaluations of their wellness programs through multiple data sources. This can include data from enterprise-wide surveys, employee health risks, medical claims data, or satisfaction surveys. Further actions can include making programs available to family members, providing flexible work policies, or creating any other initiatives that encourage participation in health-related community events.

According to the CDC HSC, communication to employees through multiple channels is an important factor to encourage participation in wellness programs. Information dissemination and awareness building is a common theme of success in the literature. According to a RAND wellness study in 2013, organizations should use multiple communication channels to inform employees of the services available. (Moseley & Estrada-Portales, 2013) Employers can use email, bulletin boards, announcements at company meetings, and health fairs to deliver clear messages about the goals and importance of wellness programs. (Moseley & Estrada-Portales, 2013) Support at all levels of management is important to an effective program and the communication channels of the organization demonstrate this support. Effective wellness programs also allow input from employees, or two-way communication when developing clear goals and objectives. (Goetzel et al., 2014)

5. TOP-DOWN LEADERSHIP COMMITMENT TO WELLNESS

Many companies have top-down initiatives, but the industrial manufacturing organization emphasized their corporate officers' and their owners' role in all of their health initiatives. According to their HR Manager, their health initiatives "all started with corporate. (Corporate) held the first health fair and then it just went from there. All of our different facilities have a wellness committee. Most of them have a garden. I would want to say, also it's provided by corporate, it's promoted by corporate from the top down."

The Health Coordinator and Champion added that "the corporate office started doing the health fair in 2008 and then all the plants started doing health fairs. (Corporate) started the fitness center and then all the plants had fitness centers." This organization also has name brand programs for their gyms, kitchens, gardens and other programs. For instance, in the interest of confidentiality, if their name was Acme, Co., they'd have Acme-Gym, Acme-Kitchen, and Acme-Garden. It let everyone know that it was a company-sponsored program.

Their HR Manger states that "it's all promoted from the top down and they provide the resources for the training or information on how to get one of these started, just like US Wellness (and their online program.) Corporate are the ones that are flipping the bill for that third party administrator to provide programs to all the associates." This level of top-down, corporate support explains how an organization with 125 employees can have a close score to an organization with 750 employees on the CDC HSC.

This organization also has health and wellness as their fifth core value. The HR Manager further states that he has "worked at several organizations and I've not seen it to this level, where we're doing the fruit, we're doing the salads, we had the fitness center. We do the community walks and we do all these different programs and for a company of 125 people, that is just unheard of."

In this study, the highest-scoring manufacturing organization stated that they have committed the resources to have a nurse on call at every manufacturing facility. In the educational services industry, the leadership team is very flexible with time off for illness and pursuing school. This interviewee further stated that their organization is committed to keeping health and dental insurance costs very low. She shared that premiums, for the employee, "went up about a dollar. We have probably the most reasonable health insurance around. I would think. I only pay $22 a month for my health insurance. Then, we pay $7.14 for dental or about $3.50 out of our check every two weeks."

The interviewee from the educational services industry feels that the leadership's commitment to health makes up for lower wages. In her words, "I think with everything they offer, it makes it worthwhile working there. The paycheck may not always be the best, but the benefits kind of outweigh the (lower wages), with the education and everything. They're very concerned about safety. I've learned more about winter hazards, walking in snow and everything, and blood borne pathogens than I ever really wanted to know." Health education classes can show a commitment to the wellness of employees.

An engineer in the manufacturing industry stated that

"We have higher level managers that play basketball with us every week."

Which really demonstrates the importance they place on physical movement. This organization also has a very active culture, with a sports complex within walking distance of their facility. As a display of leadership commitment lacking, this interviewee mentioned that the organization does not have a designated person to solely promote wellness programs. In the interview, he stated that "we don't have that person to promote the programs. We do have a training division in HR that makes sure that every year that we repeat programs and information." The CDC HSC provides a budget for wellness programs and this organization demonstrates that it is possible to score high on the HSC without a full-time wellness coordinator.

The leaders of organizations in the middle-scoring category had different ways of expressing their commitment to wellness programs. Some organizations use people throughout the company to promote health and wellness, even though it is not specifically their job. For instance, an organization in the 3-D Graphics industry has

"An office manager takes care of everything and to make sure that everyone was on the same page and informed about health and wellness programs."

Even though they did not have a specific wellness coordinator, "they make sure to take care of everyone and they always cared so much about individual experiences." The interviewee further explained that the organizational leaders wanted "to make sure that they supported enjoyment level and productivity and efficiency."

An organization in the transportation industry demonstrates similar practices in their culture. They do not have paid employees to run worksite wellness activities, but individuals will voluntarily promote health initiatives. The interviewee stated that "if an employee asks for something they will provide it, even though there is not a lot of promotion. There are various people throughout the company that promote health and wellness on a personal level, but it's not required for their job. Some of us like to run, we talk about running, kind of encourage others, but I'm not paid to do that." A separate transportation organization uses a safety person to promote their wellness programs. The transportation supervisor stated that "there is an individual that goes to the different areas and promotes wellness, talks about it, and (listens to) concerns; he's a safety guy." An internal wellness volunteer is not necessarily as reliable as a paid position. They can forget,

get too busy, or leave the company and thus the wellness initiatives live and die with the volunteer.

A middle-scoring organization in the construction industry shared a unique approach to demonstrating top-down leadership commitment to health and wellness. Because all of their employees belong to an employee union, the union takes care of all of the wellness programs for employees. The supervisor explained that:

> *"All health programs are union driven. I don't think that they would provide anything if it wasn't for the union."*

Interestingly, the interviewee stated that employees get to vote on how to allocate any pay increases they receive. In his words, "the company pays our insurance. We have a package and if we get a raise, it's up to us to decide where the raise goes; whether to the benefits or on the check." Further research could solely investigate union companies to see how companies were involved in wellness, in addition to union efforts.

The retail/wholesale trading company demonstrated two CDC HSC line items related to top-down commitment in the interview. Their employee stated that they promote "a monthly group of employees and leaders that meet to discuss topics, including health." Therefore, if an employee has a complaint or an idea for improvement, they can serve on this monthly, employee committee.

This employee shared that the organization's stated policies are "'to be safe and have fun' but they were not really adhered to by the company." They employee also felt that the leadership's focus on health and wellness in done for the company's enlightened self-interest. The interviewee said that "almost everything that they do for health and wellness it's not geared towards helping you personally. The programs are more geared towards keeping you on the floor and being able to be functional in your job. Once you left the place they didn't care if you were smoking two packs a day. At the core it really boils down to two things. One liability, having someone drop on the floor and then two, just your functionality in your position." It appears that from the employees' point of view, there is a difference between caring for the employees and caring for the company's bottom-line.

The lowest scoring organizations in the study had varying levels of leadership commitment to health and wellness. An automobile manufacturer is not conducting a lot of wellness activities at the local branch of the company. The local branch is fairly new and the only programs they have are pushed from corporate.

Another manufacturer does not have formal wellness programs. According to the interviewee, all of the programs are self-driven by employees. In his words, "the company does not really promote programs; walks and exercise are employee driven amongst friends. As a team,

---

"My design team, (will say) 'let's go out on a walk or let's all go to the gym together;' but it's more as friends. Because we're all friends there, we just go to the gym, but not as a corporation."

"A supervisor may encourage it, but it's more out of his own leadership experience as opposed to the company (promoting it)."

In a small organization of seven employees, the owner can clearly see any unhealthy or unsafe practices of the machine and repair shop. The top-down aspect of their organizational structure is simple, due to their size, and the owner and manager can be very involved in the day-to-day operations. According to the interviewee, "occasionally we do have to lift. We have to put tires and stuff back on. They're heavy. Dad's always harping to use your knees, not your back." On health issues in the company, the technician shared that "in a small shop like that, with seven people, you can talk to everybody so you may not need a formal survey. He can easily ask questions on 'how are you feeling?', 'how's your health?', 'is your back sore?' He tries to make sure everybody is doing well. He discusses this with everybody, if not daily, once a week to see how everybody is doing."

The leaders of another organization in the lowest-scoring category seem to mostly care about health and safety as it pertains to meeting the letter of the law. Their quality engineer shared that "I think they're more worried about the bottom line and putting product though the door. Like certain OSHA violations and things like that. They'll worry about those, but not really about the actual employees' health per se." The interviewee stated that the thinking might change if leadership "could see that it's an investment, instead of a cost. It's the same thing with leadership training ... you have to pay for it today, but you don't always see the benefit. And you may never be able to put a number on it." Future research could look at the return on investment of health programs, particularly if employee turnover negates the investments into health when employees leave the company.

An interviewee from the construction industry also elaborated on the viewpoint of the upper management on health expenses being a cost, rather than an investment. The journeyman electrician stated that "I can easily see how, in the long-term, you can save the company a lot of money, but we're one of those industries that the turnover rate is so high, that most of these wouldn't even be able to take effect before we have a whole new line of employees." He further shared concerns that the views of his colleagues are that:

"Everyone is too busy for new health and wellness initiatives. We don't have it in the budget or nobody has the time for it"

---

simply because it's such as small company. We are not that far out of a start-up phase where everybody is doing three positions at one time. There is nobody that's graduated into the, 'I don't have to work that much anymore. Let me focus on those things.' The mentality is that we need 'all hands on deck.'"

The lowest-score organization in the study shared its experience with creating mission statements and organizational goals around health and wellness. The interviewee just crafted a mission statement and goals for an industry certification. He shared that "we're so young. I just put together a business statement to get (an industry) certification. It was just a generic kind of statement; it wasn't anything to do with health. It would be like in your mission statement, you would say, 'We want to be the healthiest shop.' There is not anything like that." Further research could investigate industry certifications that do include health and wellness and participation rates in these certifications.

The interviewee further explained that they do not have a very strong health culture emanating from the organization. He shared that "as far as the company, there are people like myself that would like to run a 5K around the office. There's just not the top down support for that type of thing." Could organized physical activity, with a coach or trainer, have helped this individual who was trying to get healthy?

LACTATION SUPPORTS

Employers must "provide a place, other than a bathroom, that is shielded from view and free from intrusion from coworkers and the public, which may be used by an employee to express breast milk."

The fourth section of the HSC relates to the organization's support of new mothers and lactation. Lactation support, providing a private space, a breast pump, and flexible break times can demonstrate organizational support for nursing mothers. The health benefits of breastfeeding are reported widely, including lower risks of sudden infant death syndrome and lower respiratory tract infections. (Duijts, Jaddoe, Hofman, & Moll, 2010) Mothers who breastfeed have been shown to experience sustained weight loss in the first year postpartum, and a reduced risk of type 2 diabetes, breast and ovarian cancer. (Ip et al., 2007)

The lactation support category of the CDC HSC is a smaller and newer category of the scorecard. Employers in the pilot study did not have as much to say about lactation support as they did the previous categories. The organization in the automobile parts manufacturing industry stated that they have an in-depth prenatal program for expectant mothers. The company gives participants a free breast pump when they finish that program.

Employers can benefit from allowing and supporting nursing mothers with the time, space, and materials needed for regular lactation. One study in 2004 concluded that there was a 94% return-to-work rate after maternity leave for women participating in an employer sponsored lactation program. (Ortiz et al., 2004) In addition to the benefits, the PPACA amended the Fair Labor Standards Act to "require employers to provide reasonable break time for an employee to express breast milk for her nursing child." (Belay, Allen, Williams, Dooyema, & Foltz, 2013), the PPACA requires employers to "provide a place, other than a bathroom, that is shielded from view and free from intrusion from coworkers and the public, which may be used by an employee to express breast milk." (Labor, 2012)

An organization in education services states that they "don't have a written policy (on lactation support), but we've been very accommodating over the years. We accommodate." They had a designated room for expressing breast milk, but, according to their Director, "we don't (have it) anymore because it's where a new employee's office is now. That was our spot and we only used it I think a number of times. All of our employees get ten minute breaks" that can be used for anything, including the expression of breast milk.

A interviewee in the educational services industry stated that "I couldn't tell you anything about lactation support. Maybe there's a private space that employees could use to express breast milk in an office. If somebody needed to, they could find a private office." She further said that "it would be nice to have signs and places for people to feel comfortable with (lactation at work). I think that's just something that they should be in general; they should feel comfortable feeding their child."

The other two organizations in the highest-scoring category do address lactation. The engineer in the 25-employee manufacturing firm stated "we have a room set aside for that. The nurse's room has another room in it where you can go breastfeed. There is a breast pump in there and it's a paid break time." The third largest organization in the study has two lactation rooms, paid maternity leave, and recently, the husbands began receiving a week of paternity leave.

Most of the organizations in the middle-scoring category are flexible with lactation support and maternity leave, even though their policies may not be written. For instance, the interviewee from the manufacturing industry stated that "it's not written but we would be flexible on something like lactation support." Another engineer in this category shared that "there was a lady who needed to come to our facility (from out of state) in order to do her job. She had a newborn baby that couldn't travel for whatever reason.

They actually paid for her breast milk to be shipped to her baby while she was in Louisville.

Three days before the interview, this company also started paternity leave where new fathers get two weeks off.

The largest company in the study does not allocate many resources to lactation support or expectant mothers. The interviewee stated that, "although there is maternity leave, I'm not sure if it was paid. I do know

---

"They had women that were on their eighth month (of pregnancy) and they wouldn't even give them a stool to sit down on."

"Anything that's touching lactation support or just pregnancy in general, they could not care less about. They didn't have onsite daycare, there was no support whatsoever for prenatal or postnatal care." Further research could investigate the cost of lawsuits and the increase of lactation support during the time of increased focus from the Patient Protection and Affordable Care Act.

6. COMMUNICATION PRACTICES

"Every quarter you fill out what you thought about your health benefits. Every quarter the nurse comes in and checks everybody. . If you need something you contact her by emailing her. Then she will come in the next day.""

The organizations in the study demonstrated a wide range of feedback and communication practices. In the highest-scoring category, the organizations in this study elaborated on their practices in ways that demonstrate why they scored above average for this study.

The top-scoring organization in the study, a supplier in the automobile industry, conducts a lot of their health assessment and feedback during the on-boarding or orientation process. This process includes health screenings with a nurse and incorporates other aspects of onboarding training. According to the interviewee, this "onboarding is a gathering of everybody that's going to start. When summertime comes and they want to do their internships, they'll have maybe 300 people in a room. There may be two groups of 300 and maybe a group of 150 and that includes interns from all over the world. We do sexual harassment training, safety training, set up your computers and then part of that that day is to go into a room with a nurse and they do the health screening." Even though the health screening is done on a one-to-one basis, it appears that the health screening is only one part of a very busy day for new employees.

Another high-scoring organization in the educational services industry conducts health screening on a regular basis. According to this interviewee, they "have a once a year (optional) health screening and it gives us a discount on our insurance, if we choose. It's free and the affiliated hospital portion comes down and does the health screening once a year."

The third highest-scoring organization, a manufacturing firm with twenty-five employees, conducts health assessments on a quarterly basis. The engineer that participated in this study shared that "before you sign up for the health program, they send you a form. Every quarter you fill out what you thought about your health benefits; you can also use your own doctor or get someone else."

One of the largest organizations, and the fourth-highest scoring organization in the study, also conducts health feedback and assessments, although it is different from the three previously mentioned programs. The interviewee stated that he "wouldn't say there's a whole lot of feedback that they ask for. You can give as much feedback as you'd like to give them. I don't know if they go searching for a whole lot of feedback that I've ever been a part of." This method puts the onus of providing health assessment feedback on the employee.

This interviewee stated that when an employee opts-in, the company will provide cash incentives for regular health assessments. He shared that "they're paying people to go get health assessments, but they don't require them. They try to pull you in because they're giving you free money; you just have to show up. He stated that "health assessments keep people on track, but I don't think that's been talked about quite a bit." He mentioned

"They've discussed plans for expanding the reach of their wellness programs by purchasing a nearby building and turning that into an onsite doctor's office."

Further research could investigate improvements after an onsite clinic is added to the corporate campus.

Organizations in the highest scoring category provide online portals where employees can access wellness information. The automobile supplier "advertises just about everything, (though) a lot of it might be left up to you to get on the website and find out what's available to you. For instance, if you want a gym membership at a discount, you can probably find it, but they might not post it on the wall, but they did tell you and you do get emails about (various programs)."

Other organizations in the high-scoring category also use mass communications to share health information. The interviewee from the educational services industry indicated that their

"Wellness communication is pretty much generalized. There's general e-mail sent out at least monthly on wellness program and there's also flyers, but it's pretty much kind of a mass email."

The CDC does not necessarily reward a more intimate and customized approach for communicating, but further research could investigate if it should change this approach. Meaning, do flyers and general emails become noise when there is not a more personal approach.

A manufacturing company in the electronics industry has a less formalized way of sharing communications. The engineer that participated in this study felt that their "tribal knowledge methods" may not be the best way to communicate about improving the health of employees. In his opinion, "the struggle is being more proactive about individual communications. There's a lot of tribal knowledge out there but there's nothing on paper that says, hey, here's what we're doing to try to better this." Furthermore, their engineer felt that "one thing that probably kept us from getting a perfect score is they don't seem to have specific disease prevention classes as a whole.

We don't talk about our heart health and diabetes or preventative actions. It's not quite down to that level. We just have some personal health classes once a year." A more personal touch might provide better results in these areas, but that is not the scope of this study.

Organizations in the high scoring category also recommend providing a health fair every year for employees to meet local wellness-related businesses. They also provided lunch and learn activities for health and safety communications, as well as targeted training and assessments on health and safety information. This training can be on ergonomics and safety assessments for office and manufacturing employees. The educational services interviewee explained that they "have a health fair every year and they try to get people and local businesses to attend. I'm pretty sure they have a quota to meet so they can do that."

The manufacturing organization in the electronics industry "has ergonomics training that says, if you're at your desk, here is how you should position your monitor. They also help employees learn ways to hold their body to prevent aches and pains from being hunched over their monitor." Further research could investigate the costs of ergonomics claims versus training and equipment to reduce incidents.

The very small organization in the high-scoring category had the most to say about their lunch and learn programs. At the monthly meetings, the company provides a healthy lunch and then the managers will stand up and give kudos to role model employees. These employees "then have the chance to stand up and do the same thing for other employees or managers." The company also has a birthday wheel that employees spin for prizes. The engineer in the study shared that "if the birthday wheel lands on something, you get a gift certificate, or you get money for whatever it lands on. Then they'll go through new safety videos or maybe repeat an old safety video." The company makes the lunchtime learning activities fun and rewarding, so employees look forward to attending them each month.

This interviewee further elaborated on the company's lunch and learns programs as a key communication activity. The leaders of the organization ensure that different and relevant topics are the focus of lunch programs. For instance, the interviewee stated that "lately the boss has been discussing forklift safety, because there have been two (recent) fatalities with forklifts across the world. If the boss sees it online, he talks about it, talks about what happened, or another safety problem. We talk about how we could defuse it and they ask people to get them involved. It's a two and a half hour long meeting in the middle of the day and it's paid for by the company for everyone."

The organizations in the middle-scoring section of the study demonstrated a wide range of feedback and communication practices. These nine organizations elaborated on their practices in the CDC HSC interviews. Similar to the highest scoring organizations, this group conducts yearly surveys that ask employees for feedback on the health promotion programs, they deliver health communications in various ways, and they have a big health communication push around the annual open enrollment period.

An organization in the transportation, warehousing, and utilities industry receives their information through multiple forms of media. They receive e-mails, a physical newsletter, and posters at the physical site. Similarly, a manufacturing organization in this group uses a variety of ways to give and receive health information from their employees. They use a yearly survey, face-to-face communications twice a week, and electronic methods for sharing information. According to their manufacturing manager, they "make a pretty big push whenever the total rewards program is rolled out shortly after annual enrollment to ensure that employees get their HSA contribution."

Unlike the high scoring category, these organizations mention that there are not a lot of emails promoting a healthy lifestyle; the company does not provide anything related to health, they leave it up to the union; and the only communication mechanism is a suggestion box that focuses on health. A project engineer at a large multinational transportation organization shared that he "doesn't see a lot of things coming across email that are promoting a healthy lifestyle.

He further stated that he wished "they would promote some attention towards (worksite wellness) because I think everybody would experience a change in the positive direction." He shared an experience that "his personal life has turned around a lot since (he) started paying attention to (his) weight, nutrition, and activity level." He stated that when he "weighed 300 pounds, it was so easy just to sit around saying 'I gotta work, I gotta do this, I gotta do that' but when one really makes it a decision to implement changes and make things go forward, then it's possible to change one's health." The interviewee made all of these changes without the help from an organizational workplace wellness program, but he feels that the extra support can help others. Now, he continued,

"I feel like a million dollars and I wouldn't change it for the world. It's not easy to get people to realize that on their own and any amount of gentle encouragement can help."

The largest organization in the study, a nationwide organization in the retail/wholesale trade industry, scored at the bottom of the second category of organizations. The interviewee from this organization stated that employees could give feedback through a "kind suggestion type box, but that wasn't based specifically on health." He did not feel that anyone took action on the suggestions that were submitted.

He continued that "they didn't do any type of screenings, but they did have a stretching program at the beginning of every shift and after lunch. These were mandated stretches that everyone did together." Further, if there was an injury that occurred, the medical staff "would come out and diagnose the injury to see exactly how it was caused." Another feedback mechanism was a health and safety committee that employees could join. It was a panel and they met once at the end of every month. The interviewee shared that they went over a number of issues and health was part of that.

The organizations in the lowest-scoring section of the study demonstrated a range of feedback and communication practices. These six organizations elaborated on their practices in the CDC HSC interviews. One interviewee in manufacturing stated that "the only health feedback that employees submitted was on a survey that health insurance was too expensive and the company ended up paying a bit more." This same organization lost a lot of points on the HSC because they did not have an employee handbook or any written policies relating to health or safety. Therefore, even though they had some practices in place, the CDC HSC did not give them credit because it was not written down.

A very small organization in the study has a more informal method of communication for health and wellness. According to the interviewee, "the owner talks to all six employees daily or weekly to check in and see how they are doing. The owner will tell everyone, 'let's all try to work on this together and try to improve that,' but it's not really written anywhere, it's just kind of verbal." The organization is so small, that, according to the interviewee, "if something is up, the owner can definitely tell that something's up, because basically we're all family."

Due to their size, this organization does not have the resources for employer-paid insurance. However, the owner will arrange communication from Aflac and other outside insurance providers. The interviewee stated that the owner "will have the representative come in and talk to you, inform you on it, and give you a pamphlet. Then they connect you with the people that can help provide the insurance." Therefore, even though they are a small organization without the resources for health and wellness programs, they feel that their small size allows them to know their employees on an individual basis.

FEEDBACK PRACTICES

A lady took her child to the ER twice for a cold. She got a bill for $1,600 that she will have to pay. Better communication can prevent that in the future.

The organizations in the pilot study demonstrated a wide range of feedback practices. The highest scoring organization contracts with local doctors to develop a health assessment program and uses blood work to guide their programming. Medium scoring organizations have committees of employees at all shifts to learn what employees think and feel relating to health and wellness programs. The lower scoring organizations do not have formal communication mechanisms for their communication programs and they leave the feedback process to the employees.

The highest scoring organization state that they "contract with some of the local doctors, they helped us put together…a health assessment (that is guided by) blood work." The Human Resources department feels that the blood work as their guiding principle to help them to know exactly how healthy an employee is. They feel the bloodwork provides a subjective measurement because "(an employee) could be in shape and look like they're in shape on the outside, but on the inside their cholesterol is horrible. We have standards for each (aspect of health) in writing; (such as) what cholesterol should be, what blood pressure should be."

The best-scoring organization from the pilot study has their own in-house worksite wellness program. They have a goal of breaking even for this program and it is not meant to be a profit center. Feedback mechanisms help this organization inform employees of cost avoidance opportunities. For instance, one of their locations experienced a 68% increase in ER healthcare dollars alone. After investigating the causes of the rising costs, they found that "people were using the ER after work and (did not) realize they're getting a $700 bill each time you walk in there." During the interview, they stated that "we had one the other day; a lady took her child to the ER twice that weekend for sinusitis, which does not have to be an ER visit. She got a bill for $1,600 that she will have to pay."

To prevent these unreasonably expensive costs, the highest scoring organization in the pilot study has a "big sign that shows what the cost is" to go to their company health clinic. According to their HR department,

"This cost avoidance is a significant education opportunity because 'it's $10 to $24 for the company's primary care clinic, Urgent Care is $46, and then the ER is $600.' "

Each employee as receives "a little card we hand out to them that they can read, so they know (the cost)." This education practice came into being because the ER costs and usage began increasing at an alarming rate. According to the Corporate Care Manager, "it just amazes me what people use emergency rooms for."

This automotive industry manufacturer creates regular, two-way feedback on their wellness programs from groups of employees at all levels. According to the Wellness Trainer, "we have a committee that I meet with and they're from out on the floor. So they'll kind of talk to the people that they work with and then bring up the ideas for our wellness programs at these meetings." Additionally, the HR team will also conduct one-on-one conversations during their health screens. On the particular day of the CDC HSC interview, the Wellness Trainer conducted 96 health screens that morning.

An industrial manufacturer has similar practices. In their own words, "we do the health risk assessments but on top of that, we also use a wellness committee that is a representative of each of the shifts." The automotive manufacturer uses a similar employee-committee feedback mechanism to develop or modify their wellness program for the upcoming year. The HR department "formed a committee, brought them in, and presented what we were going to do (with the wellness program) and said 'poke holes in it.' Here are the payouts. 'What do you guys think? Good, bad, ugly? Does it work for you?' They're the ones who are going to do it, so we want their input."

At the less-intensive end of the scale, the social services organization from the pilot study aggregates the health risk assessment data, but "they, as the HR Department, doesn't necessarily give that feedback (individually on health risk assessment). Our employees have that option to have that feedback one on one." The interviewee did not state the number of employees that asked for their individual data.

The technical services industry has a hands-off approach to feedback on their health and health programs. According to a senior recruiter, "the culture is very much like everyone here is a big boy or girl. If you have a problem or if you see someone close to you is having a problem, then you just need to identify it and address it and fix it." This is in an office setting and the interviewee stated that health and wellness is not a priority for them because "they are not in a manufacturing setting."

7. POLICIES AND STRATEGIES RELATING TO WELLNESS

BUDGET AND FUNDING RELATED

The organizations in the pilot study mentioned five concepts related to wellness programs that were impacted by their budget. On the positive side, the social services organization stated that implementing a Human Resources Coordinator position allowed the organization to offer many more wellness programs. Having a partially funded position also allowed them to communicate with their employees about the wellness programs. The HR Coordinator stated that, "my position is very new to the agency. In fact, I started (four months ago). My focus is on wellness, but it's also on recruitment and training as well. It's not solely on wellness. I don't want to be misleading, but it's a big factor. I think that's one of the ways that we promote health and wellness." This statement suggests that even a partial financial commitment to labor can be a "big factor" in the wellness programming of the employees. Future research could examine health metrics, in terms of dollars, doctor visits, or bio-metrics before and after the implementation of a wellness coordinator.

Interviewees mentioned a budget as a negative constraint more frequently than they mentioned the budget in a positive light regarding wellness. The organization in education services mentioned the distance from their corporate office and wellness programs offered there as a negative situation. According to the leader of that institution, "we could technically start a program locally, we could like ask for funds, and then all of a sudden we could answer all of these (survey questions) differently. I'm really answering from the location level, and we're three hours away unfortunately. I think you're going to find in this region, unfortunately, a high percentage of entities like us that aren't investing. I think you need to show this in your results."

This same organization felt that having a part-time employee to manage these resources could be very helpful, but they "do not have the funds to hire a wellness professional.

We have not allocated the funds and we have not seen the value of having someone to focus on these areas."

They have 19 full-time employees and it is the smallest organization in the pilot study. Their employees also travel to their corporate office at least once a year, where many wellness services are available for little or no charge. However, it is not a priority during a visit packed with other meetings.

The organization in the social services industry felt that their nutrition scores were negatively impacted by budget constraints. The interviewee felt that being small prevents them from having cafeterias and snack bars and creates reliance on vending machines. The HR Coordinator stated that, "I think because we're small as an agency on this particular site so we don't have options for having a cafeteria, snack bar, things of that nature. All we have is those vending machines that are out there. As an agency we'll have the occasional themed potluck."

An industrial manufacturer, who had the second highest score in the pilot study, participates in community round tables where organizations share worksite wellness best practices. Their HR Manager stated that even though they are providing numerous programs, "the HR team gets discouraged when they hear what much bigger companies can do in wellness. When we go to those (roundtables) and we talk to someone at a large hospital chain and she's the director of health and wellness. They have a department for 15,000 people. It's huge and so they can afford those types of programs. Then we get discouraged because we can't do all the things that they get to. It is, being 125 people, it has its barriers. Right, but then, listening to some of those other folks (from small organizations), they don't really have much at all. They're just trying to get something in place. We're way ahead of the curve as far as what we do and how we accomplish it." This statement suggests that although the roundtables can cause the staff to be discouraged, it is still a worthwhile endeavor because they can benchmark against companies of all sizes and learn new ideas.

ORGANIZATIONAL GOALS RELATING TO WELLNESS

The organizations in the pilot study had specific goals relating to health and wellness. The automobile manufacturer has a goal of health screenings for 90% or more of employees. In their words, 90% is not easy, and it is a goal that is twice the number that is common in their area. In order to achieve that number, the organization has to provide multiple incentives and pay them for the time they are away from work and at the clinic. According to their Corporate Care Manager, "our goal for health screens are 90% or greater. In the community here locally the average if you go interview a bunch of folks, if you get 45% participation you're doing pretty good. So we really push it, and we pay them. It's on company time; they're on the clock. They're getting paid to go." There are other challenges for the sales people, technicians, and other employees who are traveling for the majority of their working time. The organization has different goals for that demographic of workers, although they did not share these goals during the interview.

"It might take ten years to transform a culture to a world class level."

An automobile manufacturer, who has been focusing on wellness for over ten years, also shared some cautions to organizations that try to match their results too quickly. Their Corporate Care Manager stated that "if you just walk into a company that doesn't have that culture that's been built from the top down all those years and then try to say 'oh we're going to get 90% (of health assessments).' It won't work. You need foundational principles (and) that's so important. There are some hospitals I've talked to that have the pharmacy on site, and they'll pay for (the medications) and they still have trouble getting people to walk over there and get the medicine. We have that trouble too. That wellness culture is so important. It might take ten years to transform a culture to a world class level." Aspects of organizational culture will be discussed in the next section.

An organization in the social services industry also has stated goals to promote their wellness activities. Their HR Coordinator states that "overall, the measurement is providing ongoing health education to the employees." The strategic plan includes the actual steps they will take, with the timeline to be completed. The interview states that their strategic goal specifically says, "four health and wellness educational sessions and monthly distribution of health education articles." Further, she suggests that "I'm sure it was written before this position came to be because I can tell you that my goal is to send out weekly information on some these items. Therefore, we're meeting these goals and actually surpassing some of them. Another stated goal is to "provide agency wide education to increase the wellness program." This goal is not as specific as the 'four sessions and monthly distribution' goals, but it is an important goal because they have multiple locations throughout the community. This measurement helps ensure no location is left out of the wellness activities.

USING THIRD PARTY PROGRAMS

Third party programs are helping organizations by confidentially collecting, measuring, and tracking the health data of employees. Third party programs can also help educate and provide best practices and education to organizations in our pilot study. The automobile manufacturer in the pilot study is leveraging a third party to track body fat and other health indicators. They described the program as "a weight loss program, but it's not a weight loss challenge like you normally think of. It's not just seeing how much weight you can lose and record it, it's a machine they bring onsite. You get in this machine and it weighs your body fat and it's very well monitored by trainers." They are going to conduct a pilot study at their corporate location, then, they plan to roll it out to satellite locations, family members of employees, and the community at large.

This organization also uses a third party group called Live Well to learn best practices and to achieve a benchmark on a star-based rating system. According to the Health Program Coordinator, the organization will "try to learn from (Live Well) and then if you do all these things, you get different stars. So we're a Five Star right now, which is the highest you can be, but there's still (room to improve) ... our weaknesses are smoking and our healthy food choices."

An industrial manufacturer from the pilot study also uses a third party program to track their employee's health data and to learn best practices. They state that

---

"US Wellness is giving us aggregate information based on their online portal information."

They also participate in information sharing meetings and they feel that "based on the fact that we've gone to those meetings with American Heart Association, health and wellness is becoming more and more important in organizations, but I think we're kind of ahead of the curve based on what we've seen."

A social services organization works through their insurance provider, United Healthcare, to utilize a program called Simply Engage. This program is describes as a "program that has employees designate different check marks with respect to measures that maintain health and wellness. They can then earn various gift cards, with the biggest one up to a $25 dollars monthly premium reduction." The HR Coordinator states that the Simply Engage program "is what helps me to be able to get people to participate in the weight loss challenge and to participate in the biometrics. Biometrics can get you up to $75 dollar gift card. There are certain things that you have to do to get to each level. If those incentives weren't in there, I'm not sure how much buy-in we would get from everyone." The HR Coordinator continued by saying that "those who are more health conscious will still participate" but that the incentives help persuade those that are not normally the most health conscious.

FLEXIBLE WORK SCHEDULES

The organizations in the pilot study go to different lengths to provide flexible work schedules for their employees. Even in the competitive automobile manufacturing industry, they are doing more to be flexible with employees. They indicated that "it used to be pretty cut and dry how long you had to be at work, but we're such a different company today. We're trying to work more towards (different) schedules and in the last five years there have been a lot of changes."

The interviewees state that the flexible work schedules create loyalty among their employees. They even suggest that being flexible is a necessity because "it's hard to find folks and a lot of the ladies that work in that area are females that have kids. (Since) some of them are single mothers...they're really focused on creating a balanced work and life schedule." This organization provides six flexible hours annually for employees to visit the onsite health clinic.

This organization is the only one in the pilot that that has created a "school day program."

This program allows "working mothers or dads that have kids going to school to come in to work from 9:00 am to 2:00 pm, Monday through Friday, and then be off so they don't have to pay for childcare." This program even allows employees to be home with the kids when they're not in school, such as a snow day or if a child is sick.

The industrial manufacturer in the pilot study has different methods of providing flexible time for their employees.

"They currently have about seven or eight or more different work schedules so employees can find a schedule that works for them and their families.

"If you wanted to come in from 7:30 am to 4:00 pm, that was probably doable."

The organization in the technical services industry has less formal methods for helping their employees with flexible schedules. For instance, if an employee does a lot of work in a particular day, but does not finish or make great progress on their current project, they can still leave after a full day's work. The Senior Recruiter explained that their managers "will tell you, listen, you had a good day, go home. It's okay. Relax a little bit. I know at one time I was feeling very stressed out and so I definitely signed up for a yoga class. My manager (said), that as long as you make the most of your day from 8 to 5, if you need to leave at 5 to go to your yoga class, go ahead and do it." Although this is not a formal policy, it does demonstrate flexibility with employee's schedules.

8. EXAMPLES OF SPECIFIC WELLNESS PROGRAMS

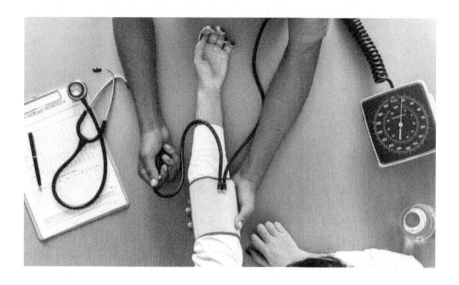

"Our HR team picks out a healthy recipe, cooks it for the employees, and then encourages them to cook it at their home."

This section examines some specific wellness programs that are not covered in other sections. The automobile manufacturer conducts lunch and learns like other companies, but they also do their lunch and learns in the Spanish language to help their Spanish speaking employees have access to the information.

The industrial manufacturer meets employees where they are with computer literacy. A lot of their wellness programs and information are accessed by a computer, and they make sure all employees know how to access this information. Additionally, they do a different activity every month, based on the national landscape. For instance, they will focus on Heart Walks during National Heart Month. The industrial manufacturer also participates in community walks to include employees' families and the community in the wellness initiatives.

There are also lunch and learns, where the company provides food along with an educational program. One industrial manufacturer conducts "cook and learns." The way they describe this program is that "the committee has picked out a healthy recipe, we cook it and then we have the recipe sitting there and it's the way to encourage associates to learn a new way of eating without them having to eat that cost." They have seen success from this program as "a lot of times it has really worked out because the employees all rave about it, so then they take the recipe home and do it themselves."

One company lost points on the CDC HSC because they did not have written policies to go along with their actions. For instance, they may be communicating healthy practices to employees regularly, but if there is not a formal policy requiring it, the CDC HSC does not award points. Their HR Manager explained that "we have some written communication policies, but some of them probably need updating. Some of them actually need to be mentioned to associates. Furthermore, they do have some policies on the online portal, but "it's just a matter of, does everybody know about them and are they up to date."

The organization in the social services industry uses weekly wellness tips in their organizational newsletter. In her words, the HR coordinator states that "I am just trying to keep them encouraged by various measures. I have these silly, motivational emails that I send out to people in the weight loss management program. It runs for eight weeks and I send a weekly motivation email that just can tug at your heart strings. (Additionally), we as an agency have also been known to send out recipes, just trying to capture individuals from different places." The HR coordinator also tries to incorporate humor into the communications so they are more likely to be read. She states that she includes humor "so it's not just the same old blurb. Whenever they see an email coming from (me) they're like 'oh goodness gracious, oh I wonder what she's going to put in this one.' I want the 'oh I wonder what she's going to put in this one' factor with my messages."

The organization in the education services industry has had less to say than the other organizations in the pilot study. Much of the reason for that lack of narrative and lower scoring is that they are over three hours away from their corporate headquarters. In regards to specific wellness programs, the location director states that

"There is the health clinic (in our corporate office), and...they do a lot of incentives and programs. They encourage us to participate, but we can't because we're too far away."

They are also the smallest organization in the pilot study, with only 19 employees, suggesting they may not have the resources to provide many wellness programs. The organization in technical services has intramural sports teams "after school and after work and sometimes people's spouses have played on our teams."

WELLNESS COMPETITIONS

"The employees were bulking up by eating unhealthy foods to then starve themselves for the competition."

The organizations in the pilot study have a variety of wellness competitions. Nearly all have a weight loss competition or they have tried it in the past. Three organizations have leadership-sponsored competitions, while one has an employee-administered competition.

Perhaps the most interesting finding on weight loss competitions is from the automobile manufacturer. They found that employees, even though they were losing weight, were not doing so in healthy ways. According to their Corporate Care Manager, "we did a lot of (competitions), to see how much weight we could lose as teams" and after the providers came back with the blood work, they said "do you realize what you're doing here?" The employees were bulking up by eating unhealthy foods to then starve themselves for the competition.

"The triglycerides had gone up at an unhealthy level because, as the interviewees said "you know what, they're right, they're just doing it for the money they'll eat all kinds of pizza.' "

and ... (then) try to lose the weight. So we made a commitment, we will never do a program like that again." The Wellness Trainer at this organization tried to set guidelines to prevent their employees from these unhealthy practices in a way that they could still do the weight loss competition. However, she shared that "all my rules were getting so elaborate; trying to keep people from doing (unhealthy practices), it was starting to get even more complicated too." They have found other ways to create health-conscious competitions. For instance, they "did not do a weight loss competition this year, but we do a walk across the U.S. (Where participants track their miles walked to see if they could have walked across the country). That's a little challenge we do every year."

The industrial manufacturer mentioned two unique challenges in the interview. They were conducting an "eat three vegetables every day for five days for five weeks" challenge. They also have a "heart healthy contest where we're having exercises each day." This organization has a corporate fitness center onsite, so these challenges can all be promoted and performed at work.

Two of the organizations in the pilot study continue to conduct weight loss competitions, one sponsored by the leadership and one sponsored by the employees themselves. The social services organization stated that "the most popular is the weight loss competition, absolutely. We actually have a winter weight loss challenge going on right now." The technical services organization described their weight loss competition the following way: "It wasn't necessarily cash from the company. It wasn't a company sponsored thing. It was just a bunch of us in the office. We put in, I think, twenty bucks for the pool. (The winner was) whoever lost the most weight by percentage of body weight." To learn more about the overall effectiveness of weight loss competitions, further research could compare the blood work amongst employees at all organizations, but that data is not available.

The organizations in the study have a variety of wellness competitions. The highest-scoring organization in the study conducts a bike to work contest. The interviewee "thought that was pretty cool," but he lived over sixty miles away, so he could not participate. This organization also has an online portal where employees can track their own health statistics and monitor their progress. The portal allows you to "enter your current weight, enter your goal, and they help monitor that process."

The twenty-five employee organization in the highest scoring category has a few types of wellness competitions. For instance, the person that goes to the gym the most in a month earns a prize. According to the interviewee, they have a monthly meeting the last Friday of every month, and they have a kudo chart. At the meeting, employees can give kudos to someone. We write down what it was for, write down their name, and you write down who wrote it."

"The employee felt that efforts like this created a family-like environment in the organization."

Another large organization in the study has several competitions, such as a biggest loser or a walking competition in the building. These competitions are not necessarily promoted by the company, but they do allow employees to use company resources to carry out the competition.

Only one organization in the middle-scoring category elaborated on their wellness competitions. According to the quality engineer, they didn't do the weight-loss competition this year because "the person that organized it got harassed so much about the qualifications that she didn't mess with it. They did it strictly off body weight; they didn't do a percentage in weights, which I think that was the big conundrum for a lot of people." The competition was not an official competition that was sanctioned by the company. It was an informal competition, ran by one of their office employees. According to the interviewee, "one of our scheduling ladies said, 'I'm going to a host a competition, whoever wants to be a part of it, it's a $10 buy in. Then the owner of the company said, 'I'll put $500 in.' The owner encouraged the competition and he was going to be a part of it because he wanted to win his money back. The office employee that organized the competition got harassed so much that she backed off of it this year." He added that wellness competitions are not something the company goes out of the way to do regularly.

One company in the lowest scoring category mentioned a wellness competition at their worksite. This competition was for the salaried employees in the office. According to their interviewee, the weight-loss competition is "in the office and they do a biggest loser between all their via salary people. You can join or not join. They track the weight loss for about a month. If you gained weight in the week, you pay a dollar. If you lose, you don't pay. If you're the winner, you get all the money."

The interviewee continued by sharing that their wellness communications and programs are communicated via email. This method of communication excludes many of the employees on the manufacturing floor because they do not have email accounts or access to computers. The interviewee stated that setting up email accounts for the floor employees "is something they're still kind of building. Email is strictly for office employees. They'll try to tell (employees) about the health programs, but not really. It comes through the email but it doesn't leave." The CDC HSC asks questions about communicating through language and literacy levels. It does not specifically mention computer literacy or health literacy, but these can be areas of future research for improving the HSC.

INCENTIVES FOR PARTICIPATION IN WELLNESS PROGRAMS

"We have basically two plans, a wellness plan, and a non-wellness plan and it saves you about 30% in your premium."

The most common incentive in the pilot study was offering a discount on insurance premiums for certifying as a non-tobacco user. Other incentives include cash, gift cards, paid time off, and flex-time that they can use to go to the health center. The automobile manufacturer provides 'credits' each week for health screenings. Their Wellness Trainer states that "if they do health screenings they get a credit each week, so between them and their spouse they can make ten dollars a week just for going to (the health screenings.) By knowing their numbers, they can enter these programs and lunch and learns, and YouTube videos….(then) they can make more money. So there are financial incentives on the way to know your numbers and to be doing something about them." This organization provides all employees with six hours a year that they can use at the employee health center. This helps the workforce because another barrier the leaders hear is "well, I don't want to use my vacation time" to go to the health center.

The industrial manufacturer from the pilot study uses "cash, gift certificates, and paid time off for participating in health programs." They also have two types of wellness plans that employees enroll in, with a 30% savings for entering into the 'wellness plan' versus the 'non-wellness plan'. According to their Human Resources Manager, "one of the things that we offer by participating in our wellness program is a premium discount for health insurance. We have basically two plans, a wellness plan, and a non-wellness plan and it saves you about 30% in your premium." Further research can investigate the participation rates in each of the two plans and comparing the savings in health expenses for each group.

"When an employee goes to the gym, it tracks you. They give you an amount of points for how many times you go to the gym, which you can redeem for merchandise."

Two of the organizations in the highest scoring category elaborated on their wellness incentives. The interviewee from the educational services industry stated that if employees participate in a Weight Watchers program for twelve weeks, they get it for twelve weeks for free. She further elaborated that "if you lose so much weight, you get a Fitbit."

A manufacturing organization in top scoring category provides incentives for participation in wellness programs. The interviewee stated that they provide free flu shots and they pay employees to do the health assessments. They also give employees a free gym membership for a facility that is within walking distance of their campus. The employee stated that they "have an HSA, but we pay $90 per month for family coverage. Then, of course, we pay out-of-pocket costs up until a certain amount, but they give you $1,200 at the beginning of each year for your HSA if you have a family.

The interviewees in the middle-scoring category shared more about their wellness incentives than the groups in the highest-scoring category. These organizations mentioned five different methods for providing employees incentives. One organization used a points system to track wellness activities such as doctor visits, gym usage, and competitions. The interviewee from a transportation organization stated that employees receive benefits for participating in the wellness program, by going to the gym. He stated that "when an employee goes to the gym, it tracks you and they give you an amount of points for how many times you go to the gym, which you can redeem for merchandise."

In another organization, employees receive a bonus for using all their vacation time. The 3-D Designer at this company explained that "we get a bonus for taking our vacation twice a year. The first bonus is for taking five consecutive business days of vacation; and it's a paid vacation. So we not only get paid vacation, but also got cash bonus on top of that twice a year." These employees also receive most of December off for the holidays and that time is paid.

A manufacturing organization uses a reverse incentive to encourage participation in the open enrollment program. According to the manufacturing manager,

"If employees do not participate in open enrollment, they do not receive their HSA contribution."

A 500-employee organization in the construction industry provides an exercise facility on site through their employee union. According to an interviewee from the technical services industry, his company "provides free health insurance as long as you go through a point system and do everything they want." He elaborated that "if you go to the gym three times a week, that's a point. If you go to the doctor, get a physical checkup, that's a point. If you get up to seven points, your health care is free for the year. They want everyone to have 100% free health care."

The largest company in the study used inexpensive health insurance and other insurance benefits as the primary incentive for participating in health related activities. According to the interviewee, "they were really good about fringe benefits, everyone would talk about how great the dental was and then the vision. They have a $40 copay which people are pretty excited about because apparently in that area it's a lot worse usually." He said that "cheap insurance was a really big positive there because there are a lot more immigrants working there and quite a few of them had a lot of children. It was a really big thing because the company paid most of the health insurance costs and there wasn't a lot that came out of pocket."

WELLNESS ROLE MODELS

The CDC HSC awards points for emphasizing employees that are role models of healthy behavior. The organizations in the pilot study have different methods of role-modeling their programs. The automobile manufacturer uses a 'brag wall,' that is a bulletin board with pictures of success stories. Their Wellness Trainer stated, "I have a brag wall. I call it a brag wall. We have a lot of people that have got off of medicine. I mean they were on heart medicine, now they're not. Not only from a body perspective, what it's doing to my body, but I didn't realize how much I'm going to save every week not going to CVS getting the medicines."

This organization also gave an example of celebrating a tobacco cessation success in front of most of the employees in the organization. This story will be discussed and quoted in the tobacco section, but it is relevant to discuss briefly here.

A member of the HR Corporate Care team performed a country line dance or 'Texas Two-Step' with an employee that successfully completed a tobacco cessation program.

The dance was conducted during a break, when many employees could watch and discuss, and it was even video-recorded and shared on the company's digital platforms.

The industrial manufacturer in the pilot study considered the leadership team as the best opportunity to role model the wellness activities the company offered. Their HR manager stated that "our plant manager who works out majority of the days, and he participates in everything." The leaders of their wellness committee are "constantly in the fitness room and promoting these activities."

In addition to leaders modeling these behaviors, they "also have the corporate-wide victory awards, which they use as success stories from each plant, we have several different facilities. Once a year they nominate someone who has lost a lot of weight or has gone through a drastic life change. (For instance,) they've trained for a marathon and ran their first one." Similarly, the social services organization from the pilot study has "a spotlight (of role model stories) in the newsletter."

PART 3: THE NEXT DIMENSIONS OF WORKPLACE WELLNESS

9. TOBACCO CONTROL AND CESSATION

"There are some scary stats out there, the last two years that we've hired, the folks that are under 21, 50% of them admit to smoking. 50%."

The second category addressed in the HSC is Tobacco Control. The use of tobacco can be extremely detrimental to employee health and wellness as it is an indicator to a variety of chronic diseases. The CDC HSC devotes an entire section to tobacco control in the organizational culture and wellness program. Organizations can demonstrate tobacco control by having written and posted policies that ban tobacco use on company property through multiple channels of communication. Therefore, it is not enough just to have a no tobacco policy but employers need to communicate through signs, employee meetings, corporate newsletter, and by not providing ashtrays. Organizations should also refrain from selling tobacco products on company property through vending machines, a snack bar, cafeteria, or gift shop.

Organizations can take active steps to encourage employees to stop using tobacco. These types of supports include stop-smoking telephone lines, subsidizing the cost of tobacco cessation medications and nicotine replacement products, and cessation counseling. The aforementioned study in Washington State found that none of the 30 restaurants/bar/lounges in the study promoted the quit line. (Hughes et al., 2011) It is likely that if they did not promote the quit line then they likely did not promote other interventions. Individuals in the food service industry can represent a public health opportunity because these businesses have a higher percentage of lower socioeconomic status, which is associated with higher smoking rates. (Hughes, Hannon, Harris, & Patrick, 2010) The CDC HSC encourages organizations to inform their employees of health insurance coverage or discounts for cessation medication or insurance premiums. The HSC acknowledges employers for providing behavioral-change incentives like gift cards, cash, or recognition for trying to quit or actively quitting tobacco use.

Tobacco control and cessation was an important topic for each of the organizations in the pilot study. In this category, four of the organizations in the pilot study scored higher than the CDC validation study. The automobile parts manufacturer stated that, for employees under 21, over 50% admit to smoking. According to their Corporate Care Manager, "there are some scary stats out there, just going through in this last week. The last two years that we've hired, the folks that are under 21, 50% of them admit to smoking. 50%. That's the "admits", you know there's another 20% that don't want to say anything." These statistics are particularly interesting when one considers that this organization scored the highest of all the organizations in the pilot study. They only missed three points overall on the entire CDC HSC.

The Corporate Care Manager stated that:

"They really want to go to a totally tobacco free campus, but that they would receive too much push back from their employees."

"The building is totally smoke and tobacco free, but we do have smoking areas. We would love a (totally free environment). That would be awesome; we're just not quite there. It would be anarchy." Although "anarchy" might be considered an extreme descriptor, it does demonstrate the employers' feeling toward the importance of tobacco use amongst their workforce.

To combat the widespread tobacco usage, the automobile manufacturer, provides a number of resources for their organization. They have an onsite tobacco cessation program for their employees and they encourage tobacco-using employees to take advantage of free resources in the community. The interviewees stated that their

---

"Employees can get a 30 day supply of cessation medication for $4. You can't really beat that."

And, I know that right now the 1-800 quit line has free gum and patches until April 3rd or something like that, until supplies last. So we always push if there's a free program like that going on, we try and promote it as much as we can."

The HR team of the automobile manufacturer shared an interesting story of tobacco cessation. The following story demonstrates their commitment to supporting an employee in cessation and the culture of health that is available, if an employee takes advantage of it. The story involves a member of HR making a bet to dance the Texas Two Step with an employee, if he quit smoking. According to the interviewees, "the nurse practitioner actually helped one guy quit. He said that he couldn't, but she worked with him and said 'if you (quit) I'll dance with you.' Meaning she would dance the Electric Slide or Texas Two Step in the break room. So she got him to quit and she held up to her bargain. During break time, she got in front of the entire facility and did the Texas Two Step with him. He ended up doing it with her. She said 'whatever it takes.'" For the research, this is just another practice to support employees. However, it is a very compelling and memorable story that stands out amongst all the other practices as a "whatever it takes" philosophy.

The industrial manufacturer from the pilot study had a number of options for employees that want to quit using tobacco products. Cessation counseling can happen through their Employee Assistance Program (EAP) and they offer a $500 reimbursement program for cessation. Their HR

Manager stated that, "I've talked to several people about (quitting) but we also have it as part of our EAP program. We have all the US Wellness programs and starting this year, the US Wellness tobacco cessation program requires employees to take four-week cessation online course."

In addition to these resources, the industrial manufacturer provides tobacco-free facilities and a tobacco free campus. The interviewees state that "the tobacco (policy) is once again from the top down. All facilities are tobacco-free facilities, not even tobacco on the property. I think that's probably the biggest cause for our success."

The organization from the social services industry has a non-smoking building, but not a tobacco free campus. The HR Coordinator stated that, "our policy adheres to a state wide, county wide, or city wide policy banning tobacco use in the workplace. But our tobacco ban is not necessarily on the premises. I would say we follow state wide law." They also offer free tobacco cessation counseling through their EAP.

The interviewee from the technical services industry stated that, as a non-smoker, she enjoyed a non-tobacco campus at their facility. This contrasted with previous places where she worked that were very tobacco friendly. During the interview, she stated that "I interned for Altria though, if you know who they are. They're Philip Morris' parent company. And when I went into their manufacturing plant in Richmond, Virginia, they had cigarette vending machines. They allowed employees to have a certain amount of tobacco products for free each week."

"I think they know if they tried to get people to quit (tobacco) while they're working on the road, they'd probably kill somebody."

An education services interviewee stated that "I feel that tobacco sensitivity has increased through (our corporate office) over a short period of time." Their corporate office has offered a significant discount for employees that certify as a "non-tobacco user" during their annual benefits open enrollment period. The organization requires each employee to certify their tobacco status every year and failure to certify automatically places an employee in the tobacco-user status.

In the highest-scoring category, companies shared that they have designated smoking areas on the property, employees can only smoke in their car, and that visiting contractors who are smoking needed to be coached on tobacco policies. Another organization had on-site police and security with extra time, and they took up the cause of tobacco cessation by passing out samples of nicotine gum.

The highest-scoring organization in our study is not totally smoke-free, but they do have designated smoking areas. Their interviewee stated that "they incentivize employees to not smoke, because you can get 1,000 health points for being tobacco free for three months or more." The next highest-scoring organization in the educational services industry says they are a tobacco free campus, but that employees or visitors can smoke in their car.

"The security force had some samples of nicotine gum they passed out to smokers; they're very big on promoting tobacco free."

This organization also offers counseling or cessation classes for full-time employees who don't fill out the affidavit as a non-smoker. The interviewee further stated that employees can complete the affidavit and get $25 dollars off their insurance. I think just along with the sign of the times."

Another high-scoring organization enforces their no-smoking policy. They are a manufacturer with flammable materials, so tobacco control is a safety issue, as well as health. Their engineer stated that "about two years we had a problem with the contractors coming in and smoking on the premises. I mean everything's flammable, with the oils. So everything has to be away from the building." This interviewee is a non-smoker, so he was not entirely aware of the organization's efforts to help with cessation.

When asked about the cessation programs, he shared that "I don't know. There's not many of us that do that, and they know not to do it around the building. We talk about (cessation) in the meetings and paying for that would help. Their insurance is through Blue Cross, Blue Shield and their benefits include vision care, health savings account, tele-Medicare, dental, accidental death and dismemberment is covered, long-term disability is covered, as well as voluntary life insurance. He felt the organization would pay for cessation, but he was not totally sure.

The last organization in the high-scoring category sticks to the Indiana state law for smoking, but they do not have a tobacco free campus. Their employee stated that "you can't smoke within so many feet of the door, which is the Indiana state policy but you can still smoke outside. And, you cannot smoke or chew inside." The interviewee did state that if an employee smokes, their health insurance costs more.

"My grandma used to work for a tobacco company in Mobile. She said on Fridays, when everybody left, they'd be at the door, giving out packs of cigarettes."

The utilities organization in the middle-scoring category has a culture where most of the people at the organization smoke. According to the interviewee, there are free health care incentives for being a non-tobacco user. Interestingly, the interviewee did not feel that tobacco control was an important issue. He shared his reference point for tobacco usage with the following story. He said that "my grandma used to work for a tobacco company in Mobile. She said on Fridays, when everybody left, they'd be at the door, packs of cigarettes. And as you walked out, they'd give them to you." He continued that "most of our top people all smoke or chew, so I don't think there's a real push to get rid of tobacco." He continued by saying that "the smoking and tobacco use is probably seen as a low priority. The law is 30 feet away from the building, and that doesn't happen. Everybody uses chew in the building, in the trucks and everything. So, yeah, health's really not a big thing. And like I said, that one guy had lung cancer and it hasn't slowed anyone down on their tobacco use."

In contrast, the 3-D Design organization was "very conscious about helping people to be healthier," according to their employee. She continued that "they covered 100% of employee health conditions." Another employee from the middle scoring range spoke of his organization's stance on tobacco control. He was a smoker and he stated that "yes, we had smoking areas out in the parking lot but there was no chewing tobacco or anything like that. They were adamant no tobacco use." This particular organization is in the retail/wholesale trade industry and they handle a large number of packages. The adamant tobacco control was more about customer service than health and wellness, according to the interviewee.

Similarly, an organization in the technical services industry had strong evidence of tobacco use in their culture. The interviewee, a non-smoker, had some strong feelings on the topic in the interview. He felt that "I think they know if they tried to get people to quit (tobacco) while they're on the road, they'd probably kill somebody. They have enough stress going on without having to make them do that. Tobacco control and stress management would basically be conflicted, (because) tobacco is their stress management. They just let people deal with stress in their own ways. For most of them, it's through smoking." Further research could investigate the possibility of offering both tobacco cessation and stress management to employees to see if they are indeed mutually exclusive as this interviewee stated.

An interviewee continued by stating that "really the only thing I could say is that they were super stringent on the tobacco. You had one place in the parking lot to smoke, a little smokers shack or whatever and it really sucked having to do that in the middle of winter because there was no walls even to break the wind on it." As previously stated, this employee is a smoker; therefore he had to walk to the "smokers shack" in the parking lot at all times of the year. He continued that:

"Yes, so when it rained, you had to walk, it was probably 150 feet or better from the front door to the smoke shack so you were getting rained on the whole way there."

The "smoke shack" approach was discussed again as a form of tobacco control by an interviewee with an automobile parts manufacturer. The interviewee shared that employees are not technically supposed to be smoking on the premises, "but they set up a smoke shack in kind of like the back area, for employees. So, I don't know where the line falls, because the majority of the office people smoke too." He estimated that "probably over 50% of our workers, even office workers, are smokers. There's no added benefit to quit or not be a smoker than it is to be one. So, they're a kind of a bit in the same (as far as insurance costs)."

Other companies in the low-scoring category do not have tobacco policies that the interviewees could recall. In the case of a small manufacturer, the interviewee stated that tobacco control might be a "touchy subject." He mused that "I wonder how companies would be able to do that ... I feel like it'd be such a touchy issue with employees, you know, here's help to help you quit smoking. Here's a number you can call. In his particular culture, smoking is not very widespread. He stated that "in our company there's maybe only one smoker, and we all know, like Jenny, she always smells like smoke. You can smell her as she walks up the stairs; you can smell her going up. Obviously a company like that can't be like, we want to help you guys quit smoking when we all know it's only Jenny that smokes." Perhaps further research can explore cultures where smokers are a majority versus companies where smokers are a minority.

The last three organizations in the low-scoring category all have fewer than thirteen employees, and none of their interviewees stated a firm tobacco policy. The automobile repair shop does not allow smoking inside the shop. The employee stated that "people go outside, out of the office, and smoke. But I can't say that I'm 100% sure that there is no smoking in the shop."

The electrician in the small electrical firm stated that their company does not have a firm tobacco policy, but that the policy can vary from job to job because they are always working at the clients' facilities. The interviewee stated that "we have some unwritten rules about smoking, just unwritten, to be sparing about your smoke breaks and everything else, but I wouldn't say in a health-related manner. It's more as far as labor productivity." When asked about smoking and insurance, the employee, a smoker, shared that "I'm not involved administratively when it comes to the health insurance, so I can't say for sure, but I've never been asked if I'm a smoker for my plan."

10. NUTRITION AND HEALTHY DIET OPTIONS

*"We used to do free donuts every Friday, but we
have now switched from donuts to fruit."*

Nutrition in the workplace can play an important part in the prevalence of chronic diseases such as obesity and diabetes. Nutrition programs that relate to wellness include policies that require, suggest, or provide healthier food options.

Organizations can earn points on the HSC by practicing nutrition in a number of ways. Sharing educational materials about nutrition, subsidizing healthier food, providing a food storage location and encouraging a nearby farmer's market are all activities that can earn points on the CDC HSC. The CDC HSC encourages written policies that provide healthier food and beverage choices in the company cafeteria, snack bar, and vending machines. Simple cost shifting that subsidizes healthier foods can reduce health care costs for the workforce. Organizations that offer less price reductions on lower-fat foods have shown higher sales on those items. (French, 2003)

Employers that provide healthy food in vending machines or cafeterias have been experienced positive effects on CVD risk factors. (Mhurchu et al., 2010) Employers are encouraged by the HSC to create a formal policy to make "vegetables, fruits, 100% fruit juices, whole-grain items and trans fat free – low sodium snacks available in vending machines." (CDC, 2014) Company policies can also make healthier foods available during meetings or employee "pitch ins".

Organizations can further provide nutritional information on the content of food they offer beyond just standard nutrition labels. One example is to provide a heart logo of colored dots that signify healthier foods. Organizations can subsidize or provide discounts to encourage employees to purchase healthier food as well as promote nearby farmers markets where they can obtain fresh fruits and vegetables. Gardens onsite are another way organizations can provide fresh vegetables to their employees.

The CDC HSC states that employee education can be another powerful tool for improving nutrition in the workplace. For instance, companies can provide health promotion materials on the benefits of proper nutrition. Organizations can also provide seminars, workshops, guidelines, or even self-management programs that help employees stay focused on their nutrition.

The organization in the automobile parts manufacturing industry stated that they provide, for free, healthy snack options by the workout room. These options have lower calories, lower sodium, and higher protein. Additionally, they provide free fruit in the break rooms at every 9:15 break. Their wellness trainer shared that "we used to do free donuts every Friday, but we have now switched from donuts to fruit. (Furthermore), now, on Wednesdays they get a Nutri-Grain cereal bar or cheerios.

"We felt it wasn't right promoting health when we were giving away greasy donuts. We still have some complaints about (getting rid of donuts)."

Anecdotally, the conversation discussed a trucking company in Jeffersonville, Indiana, that captured a 'before and after' picture when the employees used to eat donuts at every meeting and an after picture when they started eating fruit. "The pounds just dropped off of those gentlemen in this case and it would be great if we could find old pictures of when they used to do donuts at meetings. Side by side," stated the Wellness Trainer. A major shift has occurred in the organization in recent years. The Wellness Trainer shared that "for 40 something years every Friday our founding guy said everybody has gotten free donuts and free soft drinks. They got all that at break. So it was a major change when we started this initiative to say 'hey, we can't be doing donuts.' So we went from that to everybody corporate wide no more donuts we're going to fresh fruit."

The organization not only gives away fresh fruit, but they will allow employees who have gardens to give away fresh vegetables on company property and company time. The team of interviewees stated that "the free fruit doesn't cost them anything. So at break they can either have free fruit or walk over and put a dollar in the machine. Also, there is a farmer's market, and a lot of the guys, when they're done with their produce from their garden they just back their trucks up and literally say 'here it is.'"

In spite of these many efforts, the automobile manufacturer states that nutrition is still a weak point for their organization. The Corporate Care Manager shared that "nutrition is probably our weak point. We have our big AZ burgers--that's what they're called--big A-Z burgers. So we still have not been super effective at (providing only healthy options)."

"They have tried to eliminate unhealthy food and offer over half of their food as healthy options. However, the vendors' sales drop off tremendously.

"Cause people don't want that healthy food. So they go out to the (burger) truck."

The HR team at the automobile manufacturer is not giving up yet on finding ways to improve their employees' nutrition. They still have ideas for improving the nutrition options and intake of their employees. The Corporate Care Manager stated during the interview that "I just talked to our CEO for an hour and a half on Friday and I said 'I'm really serious, I would like to propose at some point down the road about having our own company, that's like Blue Apron.' Blue Apron is an arrangement where the organization makes food for the employees. It's just too easy for our employees to run to McDonald's. Well if we make it that easy, they may eat here ... but it also has to be cost effective." This is the largest organization in the pilot study, so they presumably have more resources than other companies to institute a corporate cafeteria.

They further benchmarked with an organization named Logan Aluminum that is innovative in their nutrition approach. The Corporate Care Manager shares that "Logan Aluminum is really good. Our Wellness Trainer even went there and they have a nutritionist that really pushes healthy eating on site. They have a full kitchen in all their break rooms and they have the corn and everything set out there.

They will actually cook for the employees and teach them. It was pretty neat. I think on the nutrition side that's the whole next level."

Later in the interview, the Corporate Care Manager further expressed his admiration with Logan Aluminum. He stated that "Logan's was most impressive to me. They had that nutritionist and she was very passionate about it. They had a kitchen and they literally were cooking for (the employees). They couldn't feed everybody and that wasn't the point. That wasn't the goal, to make sure everybody is fed for break and lunch, it's just offering stuff. So you smell this and you think 'what is that?' and you walk over and start talking and learning about healthy food.

The automobile manufacturers also provides educational information to their employees, in the form of table tents, sugar content in soda, lunch and learns, and even cook and learns. Their HR team shared some of their experiences on the kinds of educational materials. They state that "we have done that on table tents before. We've got better table tents now that will last a little longer, because they tend to just get shredded. But I do know that some of the soda vending machines have the calorie counts on the big square on the front. We have also used visuals of how much sugar is in a soft drink. We have put the packets there in a zip lock, next to the vending machine."

"You can get on the online portal on Saturday at four o'clock get on there and call a doctor."

Employees also have access to nutritional education from their home or their desk. The interviewee teams shared that "they have access to an online portal, where they can take their own classes. I just did one last week on the healthier you, on the nutrition and it talked about hydration and stretching and all of that." They also have access to real-time experts that can answer their health questions. The HR staff stated that "you can get on the online portal on Saturday at four o'clock get on there and call a doctor. One of the options is to have a nutritionist on that, so we're setting that up now as well. It's not in place, but we're working on that now. Where if you truly want to know about nutrition you can get online, instead of a doctor a nutritionist will pop up."

The organization in the industrial manufacturing industry has similar methods to help their employees with nutrition. For instance, this organization works regularly with the vending machine companies to make sure their employees have access to healthy food. The HR Manager took care in the interview to explain their various approaches to nutrition. He shared that "we have what we call our FitPick items in the vending machines and they're indicated with a green star and they're price reduced as well to promote them. We communicate very regularly with our vending company to make sure we're offering that. The green stars came from the school systems. There are different programs and our vending company is also working with school systems. One that they have is called FitPick. The school systems they have a very strict regulation of what can and cannot be used in vending machines."

"We have our own garden. We set out the salad bar with the lettuce, and tomatoes, and cucumbers, and carrots and have that while it's been harvested."

Their culture takes further steps to limit and even prohibit unhealthy food. For instance, the HR Manager said that "it's not a written policy, but it is part of our meetings. Our owners said, "No cake." They promote the "no cake" at certain functions and when we just did the dinner for the safety award, we made sure that we didn't have any brownies. We were originally going to give brownies and I'm like, 'No, you can't do that.'"

Beside the main entrance to the facility, there is a garden that can also be seen from the cafeteria. The HR team shared a little about this initiative, which was started by their corporate office and is required at each satellite location. The interviewees stated that "we have our own garden. We set out the salad bar with the lettuce, and tomatoes, and cucumbers, and carrots and have that while it's been harvested. During the summer we've got the salad bar and stuff from the garden. Everything from the garden is for free. Every other week we also have fresh fruit. We purchase fresh fruit twice a month from our vending company to put out for the employees."

The industrial manufacturing organization provides educational seminars and workshops on nutrition. These are provided in person by the HR department and online through vendors. The Health Program Champion stated that their third party provider "US Wellness, has probably 30 different workshops that (employees) can do. All the way from Alzheimer's to Weight Watchers. Then when we bring in our health fair, the hospital will bring information at our health fairs and other vendors bring education onsite."

The non-profit organization in the social services industry stated that their CEO, "has made a concerted effort to ensure that we have healthier choices at our larger meetings." They may have unhealthy options as well, but they do not have a written policy. The education services organization has had a culture shift relating to nutrition at their employee meetings. The interviewee stated that:

"It used to just be donuts at the meetings and now we can get a banana and a granola bar."

In fact, our culture's changed dramatically. (One employee) brought two boxes of donuts to the location meeting and no one would eat them. That shows how the culture has shifted."

The organization in the professional, scientific, and technical services industry is taking informal measures to have healthier nutrition options at their location. The Senior Recruiter stated that "we're meant to have healthy snacks. So they won't buy normal chips, but they will have baked chips. If you have popcorn, it has to be a smart popcorn. They buy bottled water, they don't really buy soda. They would buy just healthy things like nuts and trail mix and stuff like that versus something that's unhealthy. They buy fresh fruit for the office."

Part of the motivation for healthy eating in the technical services organization is to have a flattering physical appearance. The interviewee stated that "in sales, a lot of people do, women and men, take pride in the way that they look. I mean you're born with your looks but they (want to maintain good looks)... It doesn't matter where you shop, it doesn't matter but it does matter. That's the things that we're going to judge back there. When I say we all want to look nice, that's just us. We just want to- like me, I want to lose weight. My friend, she wants to lose weight. My other guy friend, he's doing CrossFit."

Even though there are not many formal policies on nutrition in the technical services company, the organization does show support in a variety of ways. For instance, the employees have food prep facilities and flexible lunch schedules to eat at nearby, healthy restaurants. The Senior Recruiter shared that:

"We have a nice, clean kitchen and stuff like that. We have two fridges just because we have so many people that we need two fridges now. For instance, the microwave is clean."

They do not have a snack bar or cafeteria onsite, but there are healthy eating options nearby. The interviewee stated that "before Chop Shop (a salad restaurant) went away, we used to all like going there. There's Shiraz down the street. It's not too bad to eat there actually, if you're conservative about the way you eat. There is rice available. Then there's going to be a new place, a salad place, where Chop Shop closed, at that location. There should be a new one coming called Vinaigrette or something, and we're all really excited about that."

This technical services organization educates employees on nutrition and wellness through bulletin boards, newsletters, and lunch and learns. In the words of the employee, "there are bulletin boards and we have newsletters that come out every quarter to everybody in the company. It's got a lot of different things in there; it's got a lot about the company, and recent promotions, like who's celebrating their ten year anniversary here. But at the end they always have something about, healthy lifestyle tip, and a couple times they have some really good recipes. And then other times it's maybe something fitness-related. We also have lunch and learns that are specifically during lunch, we provide some food, and then a person like a chiropractor would come and talk to us."

"When I was at the plant in 2014 I had actually lost 70 lbs. I was dieting and exercising. I ate a salad every day at lunch every day."

The interviewees from organizations in the highest-scoring category shared a number of themes relating to the nutrition category of the CDC HSC. The highest-scoring company has an on-site cafeteria that includes a deli and a salad bar. The interviewee stated that the salad bar was very beneficial when he was an intern at the organization a few years ago. In his words, he said that "when I was at the plant in 2014 I had actually lost 70 lbs. I was dieting and exercising, but when I was doing my internship, I ate a salad every day at lunch every day. And, of course, I was going to the gym, usually in the afternoons when I got home."

He further explained that the workplace is not a picture of healthy nutrition, but that they do have healthy options available if employees want to choose to eat health. He said "don't get me wrong, there's donuts there and stuff like that, and bagels and lots of good (tasting) stuff. But they have healthy stuff too if you want it. There are healthy options. And, by the soda machines, they've got the sticker on there that says calories count." He also mentioned that, at the cafeteria, if they have a healthy wrap, they will put the heart beside the wrap to encourage employees to purchase it, instead of getting a burger.

Nutrition policies and practices are evident at the company's meetings, according to their engineering employee. He stated that "although they don't give any discounts for healthier food, if you go to a lunch function or stuff like that, they'll give out water. Or if you go to a company meeting or a safety meeting, or a monthly safety meeting, there is more than likely going to be a cooler that has waters available. I feel like there is encouragement to get water instead of a soda. They put water out there and the lunch lady will tell you, before you pay for your soda, that if you want water it's right here." Their practice of making water more available than soda counts as a nudge.

The organization in the educational services industry has similar policies when it comes to supporting healthy nutrition. The interviewee stated that their vending machines have a system displaying unhealthy choices versus healthy choices. This employee had trouble recalling the specifics of the program, even though she "walks by the vending machines every day." She also felt that their organization's nutrition choices are "about 50%," which rewards them with points on the HSC. In her opinion, Coke Zero is a healthy alternative to Coca-Cola. She stated that "they have a Coke Zero machine and a regular Coke machine, so they offer all sorts of alternatives.

On the vending machines it has like green for healthy, yellow barely meets the standards for healthy and red is just like 'no.'"

She also shared that the security force/police department does a cooking class for the students and the staff. This interviewee previously stated that the security force helped educate stakeholders on tobacco cessation and passed out nicotine chewing gum.

The third highest-scoring company in the study, a 25-employee manufacturing company had many innovative ideas for exposing their employees to healthy nutrition. For instance, they only have healthy food available at meetings. Additionally, a couple of the employees' family members have farms and they are encouraged to bring in their produce for the company meetings.

This organization subsidizes a meal plan for employees through the gym where the company sponsors a gym membership. The employee is "not sure on how popular it is, but they have a meal plan where you pay $150 a week and the company will send prepped meals to your house. Every Sunday, they will drop the food off in a big tub. You just put the meals in the freezers and then they're labeled, Monday, Tuesday, Wednesday, Thursday, Friday. And it is $150 for the employee, and then everybody in a family beyond that is $100 per person."

The fourth company in the highest-scoring category has a full cafeteria on-site. They have a salad bar which normally has fruit, raw boiled eggs, and grilled chicken sandwiches or wraps. According to their design engineer, they "have healthy options in most all the vending machines." They also have a Weight Watchers diet program on site and they do have human resources representatives speak with employees about that once a year.

The organizations in the middle-scoring category of the HSC

demonstrated different approaches to nutrition, particularly in the offerings of soda and junk food in the snack machines. The interviewee from the utilities organization stated that:

"Our company refrigerator is full of soft drinks, and then at the very bottom, in the back, is water bottles. Also, we have a few granola bars, but most of it is chips and coke."

Water in the front would count as a gentle nudge.

A manufacturing company in this category periodically conducts a survey with their vending services. According to manufacturing manager, "there is usually always a little bit of a contingency of the move towards healthier choices." They have monthly meetings and "there's a concerted effort to have at least a 50/50 offering of fruits and vegetables and granola bars vs. the Twix and Snickers kind of thing."

The 3-D Design company is a standout of the middle-scoring group in nutrition category. The interviewee stated that "food is a big thing. The company provides a lot of organic and healthy snacks and drinks at work. The kitchen is just completely filled with fluids at all times. All the food was provided from Whole Foods and even coffees were all gourmet coffees. We verbally discussed (healthy nutrition) as a team multiple times, but there weren't any sign that says eat this, not that. Employees would sometimes cook breakfast together."

The systems engineer at a manufacturing firm had very little to say about the nutrition of their organization, however his statement was perhaps very telling. He claimed that "yep, our vending machines are pretty standard, just a bunch of junk." His feeling that junk food is "pretty standard" is also telling of his view on nutrition in the workplace. Similarly, another engineer, in the transportation industry, stated that "the only lunch and learns involve pizza."

The interviewee in an organization in the technical services industry felt that their nutrition program was not a priority for management at the time. Many of their employees travel constantly, so the company cannot really control nutrition in a way they could if they had a cafeteria. This employee shared that:

> *"The only drinks available are Pepsi, Dr. Pepper, and other soft drinks. They were selling Grandma's Cookies for 50 cents apiece. It was great. All of our choices were bad. Everything's processed."*

Similarly, the retail/wholesale trade company only focused on hydration in their nutrition initiatives.

The companies in the lowest-scoring category have less to say about nutrition than the companies in the other categories. One interviewee stated that their "system gives you guidelines on if I need this much sugar, this much sodium, or things like that. The only problem is that the bags face you (and the nutrition information faces away from you). So, you kind of have to get a chip every once and awhile to explore and then read the back of it." He also stated that the company will buy employees Subway sandwiches every once in a while for meetings.

The three smallest organizations in our study do not really focus on nutrition, although the employees did elaborate somewhat in their responses. The technician from the automobile repair shop shared that "probably once a month there's a big bowl of fruit. I mean, it ain't nothing. Dad will get fruit or whatever, and he'll just have it for anybody if they want a snack or whatever. They can take one." The electrician in the small electrical company felt that "banning unhealthy food could, in some cases, make a worse case for yourself, it could upset people, and then they want to get the idea that, 'Who do they think they are to tell me what to eat?' But if you can make the choice harder, but without them really knowing, that might encourage healthier eating." The lead engineer in a technical services company shared that "there's a candy bar vending machine at the place across the street, there are free beverages, but like coke and things like that."

11. PHYSICAL ACTIVITY AND MOVEMENT PROGRAMS

"This organization also has a basketball goal, a ping pong table, corn-hole boards, and a walking track. With each of these physical structure supports, they have programs to engage employees."

The fifth section of the HSC relates to physical activity programs in the workforce. Physical activity can help employees reduce the amount of chronic disease in the workplace. A study by the Centers for Disease Control, the Brownson School of Public Health in St. Louis, others, states that physical activity has many health benefits, "including reduced risk of cardiovascular disease, ischemic stroke, non-insulin-dependent (type 2) diabetes, colon cancers, osteoporosis, depression, and fall-related injuries. (Kahn, Ramsey, Brownson, et al, 2002). The article continues by stating that "despite the benefits of regular physical activity, only 25% of adults in the United States report engaging in the recommended amounts of physical activity." (Kahn et al., 2002)

The CDC HSC recognizes companies that provide an exercise facility on site, subsidizing or discounting the cost of an offsite facility, and providing environmental supports for physical activity. Environmental supports can include a walking trail, bike racks, and a basketball goal or ping-pong table in the facility. An article in the Journal of Preventative Medicine suggests a combination of actions to encourage physical activity. (Sallis, Bauman, Pratt, & Prevention, 1998) For instance, a walking path is encouraged in a suburban location, while signage or a competition to promote using the stairs is effective in an urban setting. (Sallis et al., 1998) Step counting activities, such as tracking and friendly competitions, can change behaviors to encourage more activity, in part because it relies on data, rather than just self-reporting. (Slootmaker, Schuit, Chinapaw, Seidell, & Van Mechelen, 2009)

Social interaction around physical activity may be key to participation. Accessibility to bike paths, footpaths, health clubs, and swimming pools have been found to be associated with increased physical activity, but may be insufficient on their own. (Humpel, Owen, & Leslie, 2002) To increase participation, employers can also provide educational materials on the benefits of physical activity. A physical fitness assessment with follow-up counseling and recommendations is encouraged by the HSC. In the past, health professionals focused on previous habits that worked for their schedule in developing a physical activity wellness program (King, 1998). A 'social marketing strategy' that includes community-based surveys, feasibility studies, and focus groups can help to optimize the type, format, location, and date of the program is effective to encourage participation. (King, 1998) Additionally, social programs that encourage companionship and esteem support can be an effective strategy for increasing physical activity in a population. (Cavallo et al., 2012)

The organization in the automobile parts manufacturing industry has a gym that allows employees to exercise on breaks, before and after work. The Corporate Care Manager stated that "there's a fifty dollar fee, but then we turn in continuous improvement ideas, we can get ten dollars for your idea. So if they turn in five ideas for the year, that's paid for. It's free." This organization also has a basketball goal, a ping pong table, cornhole boards, and a walking track. With each of these physical structure supports, they have programs to engage employees. For instance, there is a free throw contest and walking events or contests.

To promote physical activities, employers in the pilot study use different programs. The automobile manufacturer has a workout facility and their Wellness Trainer "holds workouts in those facilities, so if they do my workout (the gym) is free for them." The non-profit organization in the social services industry stated that they have employee walking programs that "start in March." The organization in the industrial manufacturing industry "just enacted a new stretching program for all workers. The Health Program Champion stated that "we also do the community walks and we did the Baby K last month where we walk the mile inside the plant. We had a designated start time and on each shift and everybody would just kind of come and join it and it take about 20 minutes to do that mile. There are some people that are pretty good on the breaks of going into the onsite gym and using the treadmill." The technical services organization encourages employees to participate in intramural sports too.

Education efforts regarding physical activity, at the automobile manufacturer:

"We include literature that explains that if you've walked this many stairs it's like going up the Eiffel Tower or the Statue of Liberty."

It wasn't something that they had to do; it was just kind of interesting to see how many people were like 'oh I climbed that.'" This organization also has a sign about the benefits of walking versus taking the elevator on the other side of the wall. Finally, they have created YouTube videos online, an internal website with information and they planned to start videos on Facebook live the week of the interview.

The physical structures include "a bicycle rack and a walking trail" for the organization in education services industry. An organization in the technical services industry has "a ping pong table in the office. For mental health it helps us because it just kind of gives some people a break during lunch or something or in the mid-afternoon. Or they want to do it maybe at the end of work, after five o'clock just to kind of wind down."

The four organizations in the highest-scoring category demonstrated a variety of physical movement activities. The top-scoring organization encourages employees to stretch twice a day. The engineer from their company shared that they, for ergonomic reasons, stop working once in the morning and once in the afternoon for stretching. He said, "the deal is, you stop what you're doing, step away from your machine, or whatever it is you're doing, and stretch, stretch your muscles, swing your arms. The protocol is nothing textbook, it doesn't have to be in a formation or a group but just a chance to move around."

An organization in the educational services provides Tai Chi. Yoga, and work station movement for their employees and the students on their campus. This movement program seems more structured than the previous organization, in that there are actually classes for yoga and work station movement. In the words of the interviewee, staff are encouraged and taught to move on their breaks instead of sitting; because apparently 'sitting is the new smoking.'"

The 25-employee manufacturer in this category also emphasizes physical movement in a manner that is above and beyond many of the other organizations in the study. They provide employees with yoga and Pilates classes twice a week, along with a gym membership, basketball goals, and a bicycle rack. According to the engineer that was interviewed:

"They "clean out the main entrance, which is a big area. Every Monday and Wednesday, everything gets move aside and the mats get laid out for the training. It's more stretching, than working out."

The owner of this company provides a gym membership and any employee or their family members can use the gym. The company agrees to pay the gym membership, as long as the employees or their families use the gym eight times a month or more, per person. As stated earlier, they have one of the portable basketball goals and a bicycle rack to encourage physical activity.

The engineer from the fourth company in this category prides himself on the active physical culture of his manufacturing colleagues. Down the street from their campus is an exercise facility. Employees can walk there on their breaks, or they can walk around the lakes that adjoin their campus when the weather is agreeable. According to the interviewee, walking around the lake and going to the exercise facility are both really social, community activities. He explained that these "are popular things. People will say, 'Oh, I'm going on break; I'm just going to walk around the lake and come back.'

One year they also sponsored a basketball league, but this was serious basketball. You had to be good at basketball to get in that. It's not like fun for all."

This league was in addition to the fun and social basketball that happens on a daily and weekly basis.

This employee continued by explaining that a lot of the physical activity is not mandated, or formal, but that the activities are interwoven into the culture. In his words, "there are some group physical activity programs, like your crew goes over and plays basketball together. There's the tribal knowledge that we can go do that, a lot of people on that mailing list, a lot of people are aware of it. But (the company) is not asking,' have you played basketball this month because it's healthy!'" They also have ergonomics training that is related more to their occupational health and safety goals than specifically to their wellness goals.

Many of the organizations in the middle-scoring category had movement programs; although they were not as robust as the highest-scoring category, as might be expected. Also, not every company had a physical activity program or commented on this aspect of the CDC HSC. The utilities organization has changed their physical activity efforts as the company has aged. According to the interviewee, "they actually had a running team and everything when they were all younger. Walking 10k's and they had a basketball hoop." However, he did not say if they had physical activity programs now. It may be unlikely because this was the organization where nearly everyone smoked and soda and junk food were prevalent in the company kitchen.

Another manufacturer in this category conducts a stretching program as their only physical activity program. Their manufacturing manager says that

"We stretch at the beginning of the day; there's a poster there of the seven stretches we do and it gives a little bit of a blurb. I actually haven't read them in two years."

They also tried to subsidize the cost of an exercise facility two years ago, but they were not able to get enough employee involvement. The interviewee expressed that "they needed fifty people to get a discount, but then we got 30." Interestingly, this organization is just down the street from the company in the highest-scoring category that walks to play basketball at the free community gym. Further research could investigate community coalitions and the sharing of ideas and how this might impact the health of communities.

The 3-D Design organization also has a strong culture of physical activity. The leadership team encouraged working out and they encouraged being active, even at work. According to the interviewee, "they bring a yoga teacher to work and we do yoga at work in an open space. Employees play basketball every week, everyone shares information, and we have channels specifically for health and even meditation stuff too." Further research could look into free resources that can be shared without a company creating new content.

Another company has walking groups that are not discouraged; however they are not an official company program. The organization from the transportation industry has an official walking route around the facility, directly across the street. The interviewee did not say it was provided by the company, but it is in a business park where many companies can access it. According to the interviewee, "it's called "The Mayor's Mile" or "Miracle Mile" or something like that." Further research might explore how local elected officials can endorse the built-environment to encourage physical activity.

An organization in the technical services industry converted their exercise room into what they call the "war room", where they meet with "big vendors." The largest organization, which is in the retail/wholesale trade industry, has a basketball court, a gym, and a formal stretching program that is led by one of the associates. During a daily meeting, the foreman would be up front and they would read the daily news to the oncoming shift workers and "they would bring one of the associates up to lead the stretching."

The lowest-scoring group, as expected, has less programming for its employees in the physical activity category. The interviewee from the automobile industry says that his employees "actually brought up the idea of a gym, the maintenance guys did, but management said no." He further elaborated that "we're supposed to stretch before the shift starts; but do they implement that? No. Does it happen occasionally between team leads?

Yes. I know there is stretching that's supposed to happen."

The automobile shop in the study did not have a physical activity program, but there work is very physical by nature. The interviewee jokingly said that "we can go out back and probably lift some rotors or something if we wanted to." He also stated that there is a neighborhood right across the street from us that employees could use to walk. Then again, he mentioned in another part of the interview that employees really like to rest and turn the lights down during their official breaks.

Similarly, the electric company is a physical labor job and they consider the job itself as enough physical activity for their employees. According to the interviewee, "there is no exercise facility, but it's very physical work in its nature. I actually go to the chiropractor, and it does cover that, but I wouldn't really lump that in with a fitness activity. The need for physical activity is a non-issue because we're climbing ladders and hanging around in attics and everything else. I guess, if you are unwilling to climb stairs, really, employment at our company wouldn't be feasible."

12. CHRONIC DISEASE PREVENTION AND MANAGMENT

The HR team "will refer them to the chaplain they have a physical problem, but there's stress causing that, so let's get to the root cause."

Weight management is the fifth category in the HSC and obesity relates to many other HSC categories. For instance, obese adults incur medical expenses that are 36% to 37.4% higher than those of normal weight adults, due to more office visits, hospital care, and prescription drugs. (Boardley & Pobocik, 2009) Obesity can affect both the quality and length of life and an obese person can have an 8% to 22% reduction in length of life. (MacDonald & Westover, 2011)

There are a number of body fat assessments to help one benchmark the health of their weight. Organizations can provide free or subsidized body fat assessments to help employees understand their weight and its relationship to their health. In order to achieve points on the HSC, employers must provide feedback and clinical referral if that is appropriate. Organizations can aid employees in managing their weight through educational seminars workshops or classes on weight management. They may also provide free lifestyle counseling for employees that are overweight or obese to earn points on this section of the HSC.

The organizations in the study used several methods to improve the weight management of their employees. For instance, the 25-employee manufacturer pays for their employees to have their Body Mass Index (BMI) tested and tracked. According to their engineer, they "do not have that equipment on site, so the company has to pay to go somewhere and have that done. Employees also have to pay 50% of whatever the charge was to go and get the test."

Another manufacturer addresses weight management by conducting a body mass index screening as part of an annual health-screening meeting. The interviewee did not feel as though weight management is at the top of their list of priorities. He said that "they're not going to have someone talk about, 'Hey, by the way obesity. Here's some stats, here's how to help.'" He did feel as though employees could receive help with weight management through the third-party employee assistance program.

"Weight management is important to us because we are sitting at a computer all the time."

The 3-D Design company, although a very active company and culture, does not focus a lot on weight management. According to the interviewee, they're "not officially talking about (weight management) but people will post things and talk about different things relating to weight management. This is one of the big things for us, even though it's not a number one priority, because we are sitting on the computer all the time." The employees were often encouraged to take a walk and engage in physical activity, although it is not specifically heralded as weight management.

The employee from the transportation industry had personal experiences with weight management, even though his company does not focus on this topic. In his words, "I've got experience in this because I've done this lately. My body weight has dropped dramatically over the last two years and all of this would have been beneficial to me. I'd say most people who wanted to do it could probably really use those resources."

Similar to the comments on physical activity, the electric company does not focus on weight management. They feel that the nature of the job is such that it is self-correcting for employees with weight management concerns. In the interviewee's words, "even if someone on the outside may look big, they are still in shape enough to do the job. I guess, by the technicality of the person's BMI, you could call them obese, but at the same time, they're able to get up in an attic and walk around for six hours straight." Further research could explore the longevity of employees able to do these types of physical careers, when a company also invests in programs like the CDC HSC rewards.

"Employees may have a physical problem with obesity, but there is stress causing that, so let's talk to the chaplain and get to the root cause."

The organizations in the pilot study used many methods to improve the weight management of their employees. The organization in the automobile parts manufacturing conducts coaching sessions and they will sometimes refer a stressed out employee to a chaplain. According to the HR team, "the provider will refer them to the chaplain to say 'Yes you have a physical deal, but there's stress causing that, so let's get to the root cause.' (Our team) all work really well together, like if I find someone that is having trouble or if the workout side is not working for them and I've been doing coaching sessions with them... if they've got blood pressure issues, I will refer them to our in-house clinic. If the chaplain feels like they're not making any headway with the stress they might come downstairs and I'll show them how to hit the heavy bag to get rid of some stress or to work out. These are all different ways we all kind of interconnect with each other really well."

The automobile HR team states that overweight employees can also use the EAP to help with under lying causes of stress eating. In their words, the success of their EAP program is that they "have a really close relationship with Southern Hills EAP, employee assistance program. So if (employees) don't want to deal with anything here, or don't want anybody to know any of their problems, they can go out there and it's totally confidential. Even when we get billed we don't have any idea who goes out there. They just bill us. It's a big trust thing."

The organization in the industrial manufacturing industry plans "to have the Weight Watchers program if we get enough volunteers or enough participants and they're onsite. Weight Watchers will still be available to anybody that wants to use the Clarksville Weight Watchers program (if there aren't enough to do it onsite.)" Their third party programmer, US Wellness, has an "online portal that has a way to track your food just like a Fitbit does. Just like your exercise you can do on a Fitbit, you can log in your food and weight as well. So US Wellness also has that (option)."

The non-profit organization in the social services industry stated that a vendor who was visiting soon after the interview is helping with their weight management program. The HR Coordinator shared that "next Friday we do have a vendor coming out for our biometric screen. Part of that is the BMI. However, in order to participate in that one you do need to be on the health plan (as opposed to being an employee but one that is not on the health plan)." The organization in education services shared that

> *"We have plenty of people that are doing self-management programs for weight management. It would be nice if we had something to support them."*

Employers can increase their score by providing blood pressure screening on-site, educational materials or classes, and lifestyle counseling with follow-up monitoring. Employers can also help provide devices and instructions for employees to conduct their own self-assessments. One intensive case management example studied employees who enrolled in a "three year program where they had an initial visit and then follow-up appointments every 4-8 weeks for a minimum of eight one-on-one visits in the first year and six visits in the subsequent years." (John et al., 2006) Through education about healthy lifestyles, diet, and exercise, and routine measurements of the biomarkers mentioned above, employees experienced "improved blood pressure and reduced LDL levels." (John et al., 2006)

Employers are also encouraged by the CDC HSC to provide health insurance with little or no out-of-pocket costs for blood pressure control medications, lipid control medications, and glucose test strips, needles, and monitoring kits for diabetes. A six month worksite-based wellness program focused on education Chrysler employees who were at-risk for hypertension helped eighty-six percent of participants "better understand and control their blood pressure and 84% reported that they had a better understanding of their treatment options." (Jackson et al., 2011)

"On Wellness Wednesday, a Wellness Trainer helps to record and track their blood pressure a nurse in the safety office each week."

Chronic diseases are the next categories addressed by the HSC. Similar to the other interventions discussed; high blood pressure, high cholesterol, and diabetes receive attention on the CDC HSC. Employers can increase their score by providing blood pressure screening on-site, educational materials or classes, and lifestyle counseling with follow-up monitoring. Employers can also help provide devices and instructions for employees to conduct their own self-assessments.

The organization in the automobile parts manufacturing industry stated that they have blood pressure monitoring devices in every break room and in the safety office. Their Wellness Trainer states that she does "Wellness Wednesdays, where I try and rotate what break room I'm at to help aide and to track blood pressure for them and then one of the nurses goes into the safety office and helps with that every Wednesday."

The Corporate Care Manager shares that they can easily fall into a trap of making excuses for poor blood pressure. He states that "The Southern Indiana area that's the excuse we all use. We have all the (bad) food joints around here, but a lot of places have bad food joints, you know? A lot of those bad food joints sometimes have healthy options, it's just the decision that we make in those situations."

The automobile manufacturing interviewees continue by stating that obesity and related conditions are "huge to us. That's where this weight loss thing that we're bringing it out, not a weight challenge, but a weight loss initiative will affect all those hypertension and all those things. It's big." They also share concerns about sales employees and technicians that are on the road and on their own schedule and environment. They team discuss these employees' nutrition and shares that "sometimes with the amount of drivers and sales guys on the road that we have, they just sit there and slug those soft drinks like crazy and monster drinks. Some guys will drink five or six a day. They're expensive. They're not cheap. So you spend fifteen to twenty bucks a day on Monster drinks."

This HR Team further explains why obesity and related conditions are so important and the top priority. Their Corporate Care Manager says,

"When I say number one, a lot of it depends how you're looking at it. When you look at it from a cost perspective and how we can make a dent there, being overweight is definitely number one." They feel that obesity relates to diabetes, hypertension, high blood pressure and cholesterol, as well as poor physical movement.

The companies in the highest-scoring category offer a few programs to address chronic conditions related to high blood pressure, high cholesterol, and diabetes. A 1500-employee, automobile supplier conducts health screening with a nurse during the on-boarding process. Furthermore, the on-boarding process is not the only time to catch these conditions, as the company offers ongoing health screenings for all employees.. In the words of the interviewee, "they will check it at onboarding and they have (ongoing) health screenings for people that aren't new hires."

"This particular organization is affiliated with a medical school, a hospital network, and primary care physicians...the organization offers something that could be easily accessed for employees."

In the educational services industry, the interviewee in this study shared that the address high blood pressure, especially in the way it relates to stress management. This particular organization is affiliated with a medical school, a hospital network, and primary care physicians. The employee stated that the organization "offers something that could be easily accessed for employees as well, because they have their own hospital and health network. She also felt that the same resources would be available for high blood pressure and high cholesterol through the health insurance the company offers. The 1000-employee manufacturer in this category also draws blood during their annual health screening to test for and address these issues.

The organizations in the middle-scoring category have programs to explore these poor health conditions in their employees. However, as might be assumed, the interviewees did not have knowledge of strong programs like were evident in the highest-scoring group. The engineer in the utilities organization stated that "they have blood drives all the time, so I'm guessing they (check for high blood pressure, high cholesterol, and diabetes) when they did that." However, he was not aware of a focused, on-going campaign for addressing these issues.

"I'm still young. If it's not gonna hurt me, it's not a problem. I mean, that's kind of how they're thinking right now."

A 70-employee manufacturer provides a blood pressure testing machine with literature on how to test and interpret one's blood pressure. This enables employees to monitor their own blood pressure and earns points on the CDC HSC. Even so, diabetes, high blood pressure, and high cholesterol, were lower scoring categories for them. The interviewee felt that "the perception that these conditions don't directly affect the 'right now.' Maybe we don't focus on this because this is something that would be long term deterioration."

The regional transportation organization offers employees a yearly check up to look into high blood pressure, high cholesterol, and diabetes. The interviewee described it by saying that "you have the option of going for a yearly check-up, with no copay, to get your yearly checkup. It's through your insurance, so you can choose the doctor of your choice. However, everybody may not take them up on that." Further research might explore the health outcomes or costs of companies that mandate an annual checkup, versus companies that only offer to pay for it if employees opt-in.

The organizations in the lowest-scoring category did not have formal policies on reducing high cholesterol, high blood pressure, and diabetes. An interviewee from a 450-employee automobile manufacturer felt that these chronic conditions are not a priority for him or for many in his company. In his words, "I'm still young. If it's not gonna hurt me, it's not a problem. I mean, that's kind of how they're thinking right now. Later on, will it change? I know it probably will, once they get structured they probably bring in some more of this. But right now, it's just they got everything laid out into, I would say, percentage of importance. If it's not getting them in trouble and it's not something they have to, on paper, provide, then their focus isn't gonna be on this." Further research could revisit these companies to see what has changed as they build more human resources structures and mature.

A small electrical company in this category does not provide many resources for treating or preventing these conditions. The interviewee described it by saying that "we don't have any official policies, but we do have one person working for us now with diabetes, and we had another one worked for us for over two years with diabetes. And they do help him through insurance." He further stated that other employers he has worked for in the manufacturing industry similarly did not provide many resources. He stated that "I'm even thinking of past companies that I've worked for in manufacturing. Most of them, I'd say, really, probably would mostly have the same answers."

13. MENTAL HEALTH AND SUPPORT

"Innovative leaders go beyond stress management and they make employees' day-to-day work less stressful."

The sixth topic on the HSC is stress management. Stress in the workplace has received increasing attention in recent years and the CDC HSC focuses on ways that employers can support the mental health of their employees. One study in Europe's largest employer, the National Health Service, found that 30% of sickness absence is due to stress. (Blake & Lee, 2007) In the CDC HSC, employers can earn points for providing a space for deep-breathing exercises and other relaxation activities. Social events such as team-building activities, picnics, company anniversaries and holiday parties, or employee sports teams have the ability to meet the social needs of employees.

To earn points on the CDC HSC, organizations can also provide stress management programs, either online, onsite, or offsite. These may include work life balance skills programs, stress reduction, and stress identification skills. Stress related issues can include changes in work schedules, time management demands, specific work practices, and work processes. The organization in the automobile parts manufacturing industry stated that some employees "turn off the lights, turn the TV on and they walk on treadmills clear their minds."

In the stress management category, the CDC HSC offers points for stress management and reduction. Some authors in the literature suggest that innovative leaders go beyond stress management and they make employees' day-to-day work less stressful. Employers can address stress reduction part of the culture and climate of the organization by creating the following aspects in the organizational climate:

- "Setting guidelines for meetings (e.g., a clearly defined agenda, a firm start and end time, and actionable outcomes rather than free-flowing discussion that leaves people feeling their time was wasted).

- Fostering connections between new and long-term employees with mentoring relationships.

- Celebrating successes on a regular basis in a way that demonstrates how each member of the team helped the company to achieve a goal and shows employees how their work is meaningful.

- Allowing flexible schedules can go a long way toward reducing stress.

- Teaching employees how to use technology to their advantage (e.g. managing interruptions, avoiding the tendency to become slaves to their e-mail.)

- Involving supervisors in managing employees' stress by regularly reviewing team workloads and dynamics and sharing values and results." (Dee W. Edington, 2015)

Organizations can provide stress management programs, either online, onsite, or offsite. These may include work life balance skills programs, stress reduction, and stress identification skills. Participants in a workplace study on online support and stress management found that "the percentage of participants who reported practicing meditation at least once per week was greater among those with group support than without group support; 94% versus 54%." (Allexandre et al., 2016) Employees also benefit by being included in the decision-making process for issues that impact job stress. Stress related issues can include changes in work schedules, time management demands, specific work practices, and work processes. Additionally, a positive and optimistic manage can lead to the same behavior traits in employees. (Alyssa B. Schultz, 2007)

An automobile manufacturer provides several conference rooms where at breaks and lunches some employees are doing bible study. The Corporate Care Manager shared that:

"You'll walk by and there'll be six guys sitting around there with the Bible out. Some of them are just in there with their head up against the walls."

A company that is allowing this type of activity earns points on the CDC HSC for Stress Management. The Wellness Trainer further explained that "we use a lot of rooms multi-purposely. If I were going to do lunch time yoga, I would have to jump into a conference room and say 'everybody come in,' turn the lights down, or something like that."

This organization also has a leadership development class where stress management has been brought up. The HR team stated that at the last class, the group suggested a program for people with posttraumatic stress disorder. Additionally, their Continuous Improvement program helps because "employees turn in ideas to reduce hard work which creates stress. We really push 'what makes your day difficult?'"

An organization in education services stated that they have the stress free zones. These zones are more utilized during midterm and final exams when students or employees are more likely to experience stress. The organization in the technical services industry stated that "there is an area like the break room, (where) a lot of people just go in there and actually sit and eat their lunch in there rather than at their desk. This takes them away from their desk."

Additionally, the technical services company has "holiday parties, team building events, or a group happy hour event if (they) have a really great week or really great quarter." This organization also allows employees to have input in decisions about work processes. In the words of the Senior Recruiter, "it depends on who you are and how much time here you have with the company. But, I would say yeah, everyone still has a say but I think once you have a little bit more respect in the pit, your voice is definitely a little bit more heard."

The organizations in the highest-scoring category have a number of different methods for addressing stress in their workforce. A large manufacturer in the automobile industry offers quiet spots in the form of conference rooms where employees can escape workplace stress. In addition to providing the physical support in the form of a break room, the culture make it acceptable to step into a dark conference room to escape stress and practice deep breathing, for instance. The engineer in this study stated that "if I was working and I wanted to take a break there are quiet places that I can step into and no one would say anything (negative) to you about it.

This organization also has a morning meeting where employees and leadership can share ideas on how to make the work processes and environment better. The interviewee shared that "you can show up at the morning meeting before they start production and find out what the downfall was yesterday, or how did production run yesterday, what's the plan today to do anything differently, are we planning machine down time or something like that." He felt as though giving employees an overview of the bigger picture really helped them in terms of stress management and knowing the overall plan for the day's production.

An organization in educational services industry helps employees manage stress in a number of ways, including social events, private counseling, and an 'open door policy' with Human Resources. According to the interviewee,

"We have at least quarterly events for employees, like a cookout, Christmas dinner, and all sorts of social events."

She continued that "you can either go to the staff counselor or HR with issues on any kind of workplace issues that you're having. And, we have a counseling service onsite and it's free for the employees and students."

Another manufacturer in this group conducted a training program to help employees and managers recognize and deal with stress. The interviewee described it as an event "related to stress relief, but it was with giant rubber bands. So it's like a stretch but it was about the topic of stress relief. Because stress can relate to physical injuries, so it was just more like releasing tension." This is the also the organization that discussed the Monday and Wednesday yoga classes in the physical movement section.

Similar to the conference rooms mentioned earlier, another manufacturer in this group has a break room where employees can decompress.

"We also have private 'phone booths' throughout the building. In a cubicle culture, this feature allows employees to find privacy for phone calls stress management, or to think through a particular issue without any distractions."

The interviewee stated that the phone booths received a lot of criticism before they were implemented, but now they are being used widely. Additionally, this organization has company dinners that are sponsored every year where a department can go out to dinner together.

The organizations in the middle-scoring category listed a number of themes that related to stress management. The utilities organization has given everyone their own office, but employees "can't really get away from work" so that private space did not help with stress management. Another manufacturing interviewee stated that "it's pretty well advertised through our insurance" that the company helps with stress management. According to this manager, most of the programs on stress related issues are self-managed by the employees.

A manufacturer near the bottom of the middle category had some interesting feelings on what causes stress at his organization. He stated that it is widely known that the company will help employees in extreme circumstances relating to stress. In his words, "I've been told before so that you don't have a mental breakdown or something like that, they make it easier on you, you just need to tell them." As previously stated, when the onus of looking for help with health and wellness falls on the employees, versus on the leadership of the company, will the employees take the necessary steps to receive the care they need?

This engineer continued by sharing that their culture of in-fighting has a lot to do with the stress at the organization. For instance, he stated that "sometimes issues go to an upper level and they bicker and fight with each other until they make decisions." He continued that "you've got to understand that our culture is that 95% of the people there, all they do is complain about something; which is what you're going to get a lot of places. Anywhere else I've worked, everybody wants to complain about decisions everybody else is making all day." Further research could investigate companies that provide communication platforms for constructive conversations and if this cuts down on the complaining.

This interviewee continued by sharing that misunderstandings between departments, roles, and responsibilities can cause stress at his worksite. He described his situation by saying that "as far as half the people there are concerned, I don't work. They think that I come in after them, sometimes I leave before them. They feel like they never see me do anything because I'm not tied to production. I'm there on a problem-solving level, but they are on a part level." This employee emphasized this misunderstanding by telling the story of a coworker that was moved from the manufacturing floor to the office environment. When this employee transitioned, according t the interviewee, "he kind of took a step back and all the sudden he's realizing how much stuff we're involved in on a day to day basis. He's like, 'I didn't know y'all had this much stuff going on' because he just assumed we didn't do anything. So, in a culture like that, a lot of times all you're going to get when you talk to somebody is a bunch of complaints at all levels. There are complaints on my team, there are complaints on the teams above me, different departments. It's just how it is."

An interviewee from the construction industry offered a unique perspective on flexibility in the work place and how that can affect stress. He described his situation thusly, "it's construction and if I want to take off, I take off, I just don't get paid. Granted, at the end of the job, attendance is a big issue. People just don't come to work. But if I need a day off, I tell them I'll take a day off. Where these guys are (taking advantage of the situation and) just not showing up." He continued that "usually you pay for that at the end of the job. If you've been doing a good job, then you get moved onto another job. You can get moved to a good job, you can get moved to a crappy job, or you can just get cut." He explained that attendance is up to the employee and they miss what they can afford to miss. However, more reliable employees have better jobs and job security.

On the topic of stress management, this construction manager had another interesting story from a previous employer in the manufacturing industry. He felt that his previous employment situation was very stressful because of the lack of activity. He was in the preventative maintenance department and rather than proactively solve problems, they spent a lot of time idle, waiting on problems to occur. He felt that:

"They say we don't want you to fix it, just 'Band-Aid' it. When you go two or three days without a call to fix something, it's like 'What am I doing here?'

To have days like that, or to have times like that is one thing, but to have a career like that is totally different." Further research could investigate the stress of too much activity versus too little activity and how employers can find the balance to keep employees stimulated, but not over-stressed.

The last organization in the middle-scoring category did offer a quiet place to help employees escape the stress of their work. However, the dedicated, quiet space was only for employees of the Muslim faith. The interviewee shared that the employer provided a room for them to pray three times a day at work (because their faith asks them to pray five times daily). Apparently this caused a lot of problems because non-Muslims did not have a quiet place to relax. According to the interviewee, some non-Muslims also felt that their Muslim co-workers received more breaks because of their faith and that they were not really praying, but using the room to get out of work. This individual also had a criticism of the way his organization treated them during stressful times of the annual business cycle. He stated that:

"During peak times, they would bring in cake pops...and made me so mad...as if they were saying 'here's a sucker for being a sucker, working 60 hours a week.'"

The organizations in the lowest-scoring category seem to address stress management in their cultures, but the efforts are mostly informal.

The CDC HSC makes a distinction in that it awards points for written and formal policies, but not for informal, non-written policies. For instance, an interviewee from a small manufacturer could only think of free tickets to the Kentucky state fair as their employer's stress management program.

The seven-employee automobile repair shop that we have discussed has a number of initiatives, although they are mostly informal. According to their technician, "the actual shop is very quiet during lunch. They just kind of chill out during lunchtime." The owner is also consistent about getting everyone together for the holidays and taking employees out to dinner on a regular basis. These social activities provide the organization with points on the CDC HSC. The interviewee also stated that the owner is accessible and open to ideas on change and improvement. He stated that "if there's something that we can make things easier, like if there's a process, we kind of all collaborate to see what we could do to make it easier." This employee collaboration is also rewarded by the HSC.

The six-employee electrical company earned points in the stress management category, although most of their efforts are unofficial. The journeyman electrician stated that:

"Any opportunity the owner gets to take us all out somewhere for lunch, he takes it. But it's not like there's the traditional yearly barbecue at the park."

This organization also worked with an employee that had health issues, although they do not have a policy that stated they would help someone. The interviewee shared that "we did have one guy that was diagnosed with serious health issues. The only thing we could do is to give him some time off when he needed it, but no, we have no programs or anything like that."

The interviewee from the technical services industry described that their boss is very accommodating on the topic of stress management. Again, they did not have a location or program to help deal with stress, but the leadership helps employees when the workload involves more stress.

The interviewee stated that "my boss, which is the owner, he'll see (stress) and he's very reassuring of any kind of mistake that's been made. He's very good about, 'don't worry about it, breathe, no big deal.' So its very good in that regard but no there's no actual scream room. I wish there was." The engineer also feels that every time the company tries to roll out a new imitative, the owner will ask for input from the employees. Future research could explore the level of stress and how it's impacted by a nearby leader in a flat organization, versus a large organization with a lot of wellness programs, but a greater power distance between employees and decision makers.

"The World Health Organization (WHO) ranks depression (major depressive disorder (MDD)) as the fourth leading cause of disability worldwide."

Similar to stress, depression is another mental health issue the HSC addresses. Employees suffering from depression can impact the organization through loss of productivity, absenteeism, and other hard to quantify ways. The World Health Organization (WHO) ranks depression (major depressive disorder (MDD)) as the "fourth leading cause of disability worldwide." (Murray & Lopez, 1996) According to the CDC HSC, worksites help their employees with depression if they provide clinical screening beyond self-reporting, followed by direct feedback and clinical referral if appropriate.

Depression can be difficult to diagnose for a number of reasons. Employees can avoid diagnosis because of stigma, denial, lack of physician skill or knowledge, "lack of availability of providers and treatments, limitations of third-party coverage, and restrictions on specialist, drug, and psychotherapeutic care." (Goldman, Nielsen, & Champion, 1999) Employers can help remove these barriers and the HSC encourages employers to do so. For instance, employers can also provide self-assessment tools, brochures, videos, posters, and other media, as well as educational seminars to address depression. Organizations can receive points for providing health insurance coverage that supports depression medications and mental health counseling with little or no out-of-pocket cost for employees.

Employees may misunderstand their depression if it's covered by burnout. Past research has underestimated the link between burnout and depression. Treatments for depression may help workers identified as burned out, due to the overlap. (Schonfeld & Bianchi, 2016) One-on-one or group lifestyle counseling can also help employees cope with their depression. The CDC HSC provides credit whether the counseling is provided in-house, provided by an outside vendor, or offered through a health insurance program. Workplaces are also encouraged to train their managers on how to "recognize depression, productivity or safety issues, and (provide) company or community resources for managing depression." (CDC, 2014)

As noted above, one of the leading causes of employee depression can be burnout and exhaustion. An increasingly leading cause of this feeling in employees are the 24/7 expectations that accompany the rise of the global company. (Dee W. Edington, 2015) "The human body's stress response system is designed to respond to and resolve acute stressors;

"The chronic levels of stress experienced by many adults today take an incredible toll on their physical and emotional health in a variety of ways."

(Dee W. Edington, 2015) These authors suggest that organizations go further than the CDC HSC suggests and "bar email messages and other forms of communication in the evenings and on weekends." (Dee W. Edington, 2015)

Similar to stress, depression is another mental health issue that the HSC addresses. Employees suffering from depression can impact the organization through loss of productivity, absenteeism, and other hard to quantify ways. Employers can help remove these barriers and the HSC encourages employers to do so. For instance, employers can also provide self-assessment tools, brochures, videos, posters, and other media, as well as educational seminars to address depression. Organizations can receive points for providing health insurance coverage that supports depression medications and mental health counseling with little or no out-of-pocket cost for employees.

An organization in the automobile parts manufacturing industry stated that they "we have a lot of resources and at one point we were going make them all free, but then it came back we really probably ought to have a little skin in the game. So for instance, employees can go see the chaplain and use their time. Or go to our in-house clinic, or go to EAP, it's very minimal cost." It seems as though there is a bias against depression or stress related illness. For instance, the company requires employees to use their vacation time to see the chaplain, but allows employees six hours of free time to see a nurse or physician. Further research could explore why this preference exists.

Even though the organization requires employees to spend some money for depression and stress-related illness, they do not turn anyone away due to the cost. Their Corporate Care Manager states that "there is a sliding scale so if somebody can't afford it they're going to make sure that they can afford it. Here with us if we have an issue we'll figure a way out to help the person.

> *"We never turn anybody away from our onsite clinic. Ever. That's not a profit center. We break even. Our budget is to break even."*

An organization in the industrial manufacturing industry also has an EAP program that can help employees with depression issues. However, the EAP and depression resources may not be shared as widely as the HR Team feels the information is or should be shared. According to the interviewees, "it's posted on the bulletin board right now about our EAP. It's not a well-utilized benefit. So we could probably bump up our presentations on that. It's part of the new hire presentation but if you've been here 20 years, you've forgotten that."

An organization in education services states that "absolutely, we have services for depression screening. We are on it. Basically, if someone asks for it, (we) would do anything, but it's not necessarily in your face unless you were probably at the corporate office, because they've got that clinic. The clinic does everything. They're constantly running programs. We hear about it ... and they've got the....recreation center... I mean, (corporate office) has got it together but we unfortunately (do not.)" The interviewee did not comment on how many employees ask for it or if there are any announcements regarding depression tools. The non-profit organization in the social services industry also has an EAP program. The HR Coordinator stated that "I want to say the answer is yes, we have depression tools. That information is through the EAP and then any of the wellness information that we send out."

An organization in the technical services industry stated that their culture is very 'hands-off' when it comes to depression. The Senior Recruiter feels that "the culture is very much like everyone here is a big boy or girl. If you have a problem or if you see someone close to you having a problem then you just need to identify it and address it and fix it." Future studies could explore the reasons companies focus heavily on some aspects of the CDC HSC, but then are very hands off on other aspects.

Several companies lumped depression into other emotional difficulties, such as drug use, domestic problems, and financial worries.

The organizations in the highest-scoring categories have similar strategies for addressing depression in their workforce. In the educational services industry, employees are offered classes on treating depression. They can also sign-up for one-on-one or group lifestyle counseling. Another organization has a quarterly questionnaire quiz where they survey employees on many aspects of health and wellness. The interviewee stated that "they don't actually go into detail on depression, it is (just) a little checkbox.....we've never had that happen. I don't know anyone that's ever expressed that need... I mean we're so small it's just everybody kind of knows everything." Further research could look at these smaller companies to see if "everybody really does know everything" or if extra efforts could help uncover mental health issues in the workforce.

A large manufacturer in this category offers hotlines and assistance programs for drug use and depression. During the interview, their engineer found the verbiage on the Employee Assistance Program website that addresses depression and other mental health issues. He described it as "an employee systems program that provides professional help to associates in the area and their immediate family members who have personal problems such as emotional difficulties, marital, alcohol and drug, family conflict, stress, relationship, finance and legal." Interestingly, the CDC HSC provides depression with its own category, but several companies lumped depression into other emotional difficulties, such as drug use, domestic problems, and financial worries.

Organizations in the middle-scoring category discussed depression as an aspect of worksite wellness they feel is important. However, like the highest-scoring organizations, depression does not seem to attract the same attention as physical activity or tobacco control. The utility company from the study does not conduct a depression screening, but their national office does send out a lot of pamphlets on depression.

A manufacturer in this category also expressed that depression is not the highest of their wellness initiatives. The interviewee stated that "depression might be picked up in a yearly physical, but other than that, it really isn't addressed. The only thing about (the yearly physical) is that it's optional. I mean, as a manager, if I notice somebody for whatever reason is feeling blue or whatever, had a death in the family, I have a pamphlet I can give them." Further research could investigate how often this company, or other companies, actually hand out their depression material. Additionally, a researcher could investigate the amount of money spent on depression issues in companies with a specific depression-management program, versus companies that do not have these programs.

Similarly, a 3-D Design organization respects the emotional health of their employees, but they do not have a specific program to address depression. The interviewee stated that "I remember there were some of us that there were dealing with some struggles in their personal lives and then we would talk about things and help each other. She continued that this was especially helpful during issues like divorce and break ups." She explained that the "company never really talked about depression, but definitely when someone goes through a tough situation or circumstances, they always accommodate and make sure that everyone is well supported." As previously stated, a more formal approach probably makes a stronger statement.

Only one organization in the lowest scoring category elaborated on the topic of depression management. The interviewee stated that "besides our HR department, which you can talk too, there's really no significant group that deals with emotions. In conclusion, depression can be concealed as employee burn-out. Further research could investigate incidences of depression and resource allocation in organizations that are extremely busy, going through a merger, or laying off employees.

14. RESPONSE TO HEART ATTACK AND STROKE

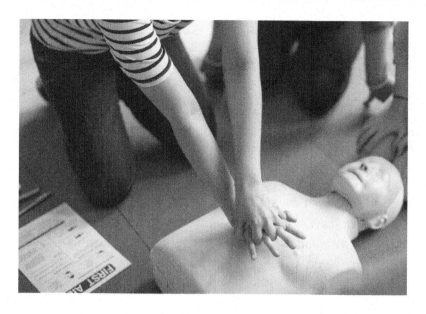

"Three years ago our maintenance guy did collapse. He turned blue and they did CPR on him and shocked him twice and brought him back. The members of the team received the Save Award. I have a picture in my office of him holding his granddaughter."

In addition to chronic diseases and lifestyle issues, the HSC focuses on acute and emergency health preparedness. The CDC HSC encourages participants to receive training and be aware of the signs and symptoms of heart attack and stroke. This includes posters or flyers in common areas that convey heart attacks and strokes are as emergencies. Additionally, the flyers and posters should help employees learn the warning signs of heart attack and stroke. Employers can share this information through emails, newsletters, standing meetings, websites, and face-to-face classes.

The CDC HSC awards points if there is an adequate number of AEDs such that any person can reach an AED within three to five minutes of an emergency. Routine maintenance should be conducted on all the AED units, as well as signs and posters pointing to the location of AEDs. Organizations are encouraged to communicate their emergency response plans to local first responders, notifying them of the plan that is in place.

Along with increased awareness, the HSC encourages employees to have a plan for dealing with heart attacks and strokes when they happen. The emergencies examined in the CDC HSC are incidence of heart attack and stroke. The CDC HSC suggests that organizations include a plan and a response team to emergencies of heart attack and stroke. This may include offering courses in cardiopulmonary resuscitation (CPR) and automated external defibrillator (AED) usage. Employers are recommended have a written policy stating that a trained individual must be on staff at all times.

"On a day shift I think we have twenty-nine employees on the floor that are first aid, CPR, first responders, Emergency Medical Technicians."

The Journal of Prehospital Emergency Care defines an emergency plan in a similar way. Their definition form 2007 predates the HSC by five years, but its recommendations align with the HSC on emergency plans. The Journal states that: "establishing an effective communication system, training of anticipated responders in cardiopulmonary resuscitation and AED use, access to an AED for early defibrillation, acquisition of necessary emergency equipment, coordination, and integration of on-site responder and AED programs with the local emergency medical services system, and practice and review of the response plan."(Drezner et al., 2007)

A 2007 publication in the Official Journal of the American Society for Preventive Cardiology studied 158 recreational service departments (health and fitness facilities). They found that almost all had "written emergency plans, but only 50% posted their plans and only 27% performed the recommended quarterly emergency drills." (Herbert et al., 2007) For instance, workplaces should have an emergency response plan, a team in place, and prior training on CPR and AED usage. In the above study, 73% had an AED, but only 6% reported using it in an emergency. (Herbert et al., 2007) Interestingly, a study of AED distribution and cardiac emergency preparedness in Michigan found that "all 133 schools that responded (71% response rate) had AEDs. However, students from racial minority groups had significantly fewer AEDs than schools with less racial diversity." (White et al., 2016) Furthermore, schools where more students were eligible for free and reduced lunch were "less likely to have a cardiac emergency response plan and demonstrated less frequent AED maintenance." (White et al., 2016) Although this study examined public high schools, it may have relevance to workplaces with similar SES statuses.

An organization in the automobile parts manufacturing industry stated that they have a team that is rated by the state through a program called "Operation Mandate." The Corporate Care Manager states that "they respond in the case of emergencies at the facility. On a day shift I think we have twenty-nine employees on the floor that are first aid, CPR, first responders, Emergency Medical Technicians." He further explained the importance of this to their organization, "All our teams are way over what we need for the certification. We do that on purpose. So, there are twenty-nine people that are on this team and we might need seven."

"The team just saved a sixteen year old girl over at South Ridge. She fell down playing volleyball. She collapsed. She was having a heart valve problem and our janitor was trained. He ran over and got the defibrillator, hooked her up, and saved her life."

The HR Team from the automobile manufacturing industry further emphasized the importance of safety initiative at their facility. In the interview, they demonstrated this with two real-life stories. The team shared that "three years ago our maintenance guy did collapse. He turned blue and they did CPR on him and shocked him twice and brought him back. The members of the team received the Save Award. I have a picture in my office hanging up. He showed up with his granddaughter, holding his granddaughter." In the second story, the results of their extra mile emergency response training helped in the community. The Corporate Care manager stated that "the team just saved a sixteen year old girl over at South Ridge. She fell down playing volleyball. She collapsed. She was having a heart valve problem and our janitor was trained. He ran over and got the defibrillator, hooked her up, and saved her life."

The non-profit organization in the social services industry stated that they "take health and safety, specifically safety, very serious here. For the most part, almost all of us have to be First Aid and CPR certified." The organization in the education services industry states that "we have a committee for emergency response for medical emergencies. We have an active program to encourage vigilance in the workplace. We've encouraged lots of dialog over the years with respect to safety and security."

Medium and large organizations in the study scored perfectly in the emergency response categories. Many of the interviewees felt the reason for the high scores were due to legal requirements. The large automobile manufacturer has emergency response teams at every facility, they provide intermittent training with CPR, and they are trained with defibrillators. The educational services industry offers CPR and first aid classes, but they lost points in the CDC HSC by not specifically having signage out relating to these emergency situations.

A 25-employee manufacturer in this category stated that they had AED and CPR signs and posters. The engineer in the study shared that "we all had to go through this training and it was all paid by the company." He said that the nurse and a crew came into the organization and provided this training. Another manufacturer, with 1000 employees, shared that they have defibrillators and medical stations throughout the plant. The interviewee also shared that they have trained first responders "in the instance that someone is having a heart attack, which has literally happened. Within the last twelve months someone was having a heart attack. First responders all carry radios and when any first responder hears that someone is having these signs and symptoms, they have their medical kit, they can attend to people." The cost and contents of the medical kits could provide interesting information for other companies.

"The organization has younger employees that they feel are not as high of a risk for heart attack or stroke; so it isn't a focus."

Organizations in the middle-scoring category have plans for emergency response, with the exception of the organization in the 3-D Design and technical services industry. This organization, as previously stated, has younger employees so they do not feel that they have a demographic of individuals that are as high of a risk as a company filled with baby-boomers, for instance. Furthermore, this organization is not in the manufacturing or transportation industry, so they are not required by law or OSHA to focus on emergency responses to heart attack and stroke. The interviewee from this organization did not state that there was no plan, just that she was not aware of a plan. For the purposes of this study, or the purposes of a real-life emergency, there might as well not be a plan if the average employee is not aware of it. In her words, she said "a written injury prevention plan? I don't remember. I never really paid attention to those things." This implies that there was no emphasis because she had a lot to say on many other aspects of the HSC. If the organization focused on heart attack and stroke, it seems as though she would have known.

Other organizations in the middle-scoring category place importance on having a plan for the emergency response to heart attacks and strokes. The 70-employee manufacturer has a policy that everyone in management has ERT training. A regional transportation company requires that the entire leadership team is trained in CPR and AED usage, so there is always someone at the worksite with that training.

An engineer in a 100-employee manufacturing firm provided two interesting stories to emphasize the importance of an emergency response plan. He was not aware of a clear emergency response plan, but he felt that "there's probably discussion about it. It's not a frequent thing, but I know one guy thought he had a heart attack and called an ambulance himself and just left work. He said, 'I'm having a heart attack,' and walked out the door and got in the ambulance and left. I think there was a little bit of a discussion after that, but not a planned thing."

"My uncle's dad had a heart attack and died at work. They went back on the videos, he was moving his arm all day, he called his wife, said he wasn't feeling good. He eventually crashed and burned in the back. Someone found him like 8 minutes later."

This interviewee stated that people have had heart attacks in the plant. He continued by stating that "my uncle's dad had a heart attack and died. They went back on the videos and he was moving his arm all day and he had complained about it. He had called his wife and said he wasn't feeling good, sick to his stomach, and he was going to come home and lay down. He eventually crashed and burned in the back. Someone found him like 8 minutes later." Further research could investigate if employees, their family members, or their coworkers would take a different course of action when the signs and symptoms of heart attacks and strokes are widely discussed and coupled with a plan of action.

A 2500-employee organization in the retail/wholesale trade industry has a thorough plan that addresses heart attacks and strokes. They usually have two people working on any shift trained in addressing the emergency response to heart attack and stroke. The interviewee described it by saying that "basically if you dropped, which happened on occasion, especially during Ramadan when employees weren't eating, they would bring a wheelchair out there to come get you and take you to the on-site clinic." He continued by explaining that the company medics would assess employees and decide whether or not they needed to call an ambulance. He explained that "they had a set of strict criteria on what necessitated an ambulance call. With that many people, at least once a week, people would drop." The interviewee did not define "drop" or the severity of those instances.

An employee in the technical services industry, with 125 employees, shared a story that displayed the dangers of not having an emergency response plan. The interviewee stated that "an employee was having health issues and he told them about the issues and then they asked him if he could go out to site anyway." In the interviewee's words, "he ended up going out there and he had a seizure or something out on the floor. He was underneath the conveyor and they found him a few hours after it happened. He hasn't worked since then and now has (some kind of) a disability as a result."

"We're all fairly young so it's never come up... it'd be kind of weird for them to give us a talk about heart ... is it heart disease or heart failure?"

Four of the organizations in the lowest-scoring category elaborated on the answers relating to emergency response to heart attack and stroke. A 450-employee automobile manufacturer requires their maintenance crew to hold a certain level of emergency preparedness. Their supervisors routinely go through training in case an emergency were to happen on the floor. According to the interviewee, there are actual trainings for certain individuals, but not every operator. It is training for the lead roles only.

A manufacturing enterprise with 160-employees, stated that they do not focus on emergency preparedness. The interviewee, a young designer in his early twenties, stated that "I don't think there's really that need for that ... just looking at the employees that work there, we're all fairly young so it's never come up... it'd be kind of weird for them to give us a talk about heart ... is it heart disease or heart failure?" Further research could specifically investigate age-related issues and emergency response plans in organizations.

A manufacturer with 43 employees in this category has five people that are certified first responders in their organization. According to the interviewee, "I think that (training) is actually overdue and we'd have to renew it now. I think that's something you have to renew every year, but yeah, we have done that." The CDC awards points on the wellness activities having happened in the last twelve months, so the certifications and trainings need to be current in order to receive points on the HSC.

The lowest-scoring organization in the study is a 13-employee company in the technical services industry. They do not have an emergency response plan in place, but the interviewee did feel as though it is a good idea and worth pursuing. He described the situation by saying "there's not a plan now, but I saw an advertisement on an AED device. I thought, you know what, we really need to have one of those because that could be the life-saving tool if somebody had a heart attack. He stated that "I haven't approached the boss about it because I know there's a cost associated with it. Now's not the time of the year to ask him. Usually November is a really good time." Further research might specifically investigate how budget constraints affect the implementation of workplace wellness initiatives.

15. OCCUPATIONAL HEALTH AND SAFETY

"Supervisors are not allowed to ever blame the associate and that's part of our standard."

The CDC looks at occupational health and safety issues that help organizations prevent injuries. This includes organizations listing safety as a primary objective in their mission statement, employing or contracting a safety professional, and encouraging the reporting of near misses. The literature is reviewed to explore programs for obtaining employee input on hazardous materials, investigating the root causes of injuries, and educational programs on health and safety.

According to the Journal of Occupational and Environmental Medicine, "Occupational health and safety encompasses efforts that prevent injury or illness due to workplace specific exposures, by conducting safety training, environmental modification, and the provision of and use of personal protective equipment." (Hymel et al., 2011) Many employers do see the benefit in health and wellness programs, but the literature suggests that they do not believe it is their responsibility; however they perceive safety programs as a key responsibility. (Linnan, Weiner, Graham, &

Emmons, 2007) If organizations can begin to see wellness programs in a similar light as they see OSHA, workplace wellness can be more widespread.

An organization in the automobile parts manufacturing industry stated that they have several occupational nurses at each facility. They are certified as a "Voluntary Protection Program (VPP) five star facility, which is the highest level they give out through the state. The state has a cooperative program, if you go on the website called VVP, and you'll look us up. There are only 69 that have that level and we're two of them." They have a new goal to become a Power Drive facility. In the words of their HR Team, "our goal in September is that we have a Power Drive facility ... it's a very high, prestigious program. It mandates that you have all your protocols in place, and your programs, and your training, and those things."

Part of their success in understanding and treating injuries is a focus on the problem, not a focus on the people as the problem. According to their team, "(Supervisors) are not allowed to ever blame the associate and that's part of our standard." They can never say "they need to pay more attention." The Corporate Care Manager told a story of another organization that shamed their employee after he admitted to a reportable injury. He shared that, "I went to a coal mine one time, and you walked in and they had how many man hours injury free, and a guy got hurt and they'd put his name up there. I said, 'is that what I think it is?'" It was implied that the manager felt as though shaming an employee is not a best practice for increased safety awareness.

"At our last town hall meeting, we rolled out our new stretching program, which is to help decrease the number of injuries or accidents."

An industrial manufacturer also participates in the aforementioned VPP program. Their HR Manager stated that "we are certified through OSHA's VPP site, which is voluntary protection program. We meet the standards for that and we're certified for a three-year period. It just says that we meet all of OSHA's regulations and then we also go above and beyond many of them and we have lower benchmark numbers on our health and safety. So our (injury) rates are lower than our competitors or other companies." This organization also just stared a new ergonomics program to help prevent injuries. The interviewees stated that "at our last town hall meeting, we rolled out our new stretching program, which is to help decrease the number of injuries or accidents."

A social services organization treats safety as a top priority because their government funding depends on their adherence to OSHA standards. Their HR Coordinator feels that "the agency is held to high standards with respect to ensuring that we meet OSHA standards. It's necessary for us to reduce and eliminate risks agency wide. Some of our funding is government tied. Being compliant with governmental policies is essential. Not that we would not do it just because we were getting the funding. We want to be compliant overall."

The organization in education services has a safety committee. The organization in the technical services industry does not focus on OSHA issues because they feel "it's not really required in an office setting." When asked if they have safety programs, the Senior Recruiter said, "No, nothing that's mandatory. However we will offer things like standing desks. "We also have headsets that you can order so that you don't have (bend your neck) with your phone."

"We have a monthly safety meeting where managers bring up stuff that they heard about on the news or at another company and how to prevent it."

The category of occupational health and safety yielded similar results as the emergency response and preparedness category in each of the three high-scoring categories. The organizations in the highest scoring category emphasized occupational health and safety as integral to their worksite wellness activities. The 1500-employee automobile supplier stated that emergency response teams (ERT's) are on staff at every facility, every day. They are trained regularly in CPR and with defibrillators. Similarly, the educational services industry requires all employees to engage in trainings on occupational health and safety annually.

A 25-employee manufacturer in this category described his organization's monthly safety meetings where many of the issues in the CDC HSC are covered with the entire group of employees. The interviewee described his company's monthly safety meeting by stating that "the managers stand up and go through everything in the department. They also bring up stuff that they heard about on the news or something that happened at another company, and how can we prevent that at our company."

He continued that the nature of their business requires that they adhere to a high level of occupational health and safety regulations. They are not only held to all the OSHA regulations, but also by the Food and Drug Administration regulations. He stated that the company has learned to adapt to these regulations and that "every new policy they bring in, we just go with it and learn. For instance we just got, about three months ago, we got considered a hazardous shipping company." Although this company seemed to go above and beyond in the health and wellness areas of the CDC HSC, especially for their size, it seems as though they have no choice but to maintain the highest level of adherence in occupational health and safety.

A utility company in the middle-scoring category takes workplace safety very seriously at all levels of their organization, according to the engineer that volunteered for this study. He stated that "our safety guy that comes around, he actually got burnt. Or they call it getting burnt, when you touch a live wire. He actually lost his whole left arm and he has an artificial hand. He's our safety guy. He takes it real serious." The organization recently held AED and CPR training, and they were informed that, nationwide, there were eight linemen die in January. Because all of his coworkers are linemen or work closely with linemen, this news is extremely relevant to safety in his immediate workplace. He continued that "the job is dangerous for the majority of our employees. They take it very seriously, so they focus a lot on safety and making sure that everybody's safe. Our nationwide and statewide offices really do a good job on health and wellness pamphlets. But locally, I would say just they focus mainly on safety."

"Multiple organizations within walking distance have a health and/or safety fair. A community coalition could see how resources can be combined."

A 70-person manufacturer in the middle-scoring category stated that the occupational health and safety is "really our number one goal. There's even a big banner on the outside of the building that says this." They encourage the reporting of injuries and near misses. The manufacturing manager stated that "we've had near miss reports that anybody can just go pull an injury sheet and fill it out, and then it gets turned into the lead board." This organization has a safety fair periodically where vendors come into their facility and set up booths. The interviewee stated that "there are twelve or fifteen vendors that'll come in and just promote whatever they're promoting related to occupational health and safety." Three organizations in the study have mentioned a health and/or safety fair. All three of these organizations are within walking distance of each other and other organizations in the study. A community coalition could be the result of further research and several more organizations could benefit from the efforts already underway.

An organization in the transportation industry also felt that safety had to be priority because the nature of their industry is dangerous. The interviewee stated that "it's such a safety sensitive job you have to (make it a priority). We don't work in a controlled environment so you have to focus on health and safety." Further research could look at the minimum requirements for occupational health and safety, and if regulatory boards are requiring enough from industry stakeholders. So many organizations in this study are taking their lead from OSHA boards, therefore a researcher could determine if they were doing enough.

"Having a standing desk would be beneficial to me because I was starting to have some back problems and leg pain from sitting."

Another employee in the transportation industry described his company's occupational health and safety efforts in an office setting. He shared that "having a desk that I can stand up at would be beneficial to me because I was starting to have some back problems and leg pain because my legs were always under a desk. I suggested that they let me look into that. They went out and procured a standing desk, a mat, and everything that went with it, for me."

He contrasted this with other companies where he worked that tried to side step the basic OSHA regulations. He shared that he "worked throwing freight on a conveyor belt and there's two instances. One, a pallet come off the top, 12 feet out of the air and hit me in the shin. It could have broken my leg, it didn't, thankfully, but I just walked it off. I reported it and everything, but basically everybody looked at me like I was crazy for reporting it. That wasn't at where I work now, but that just turned my stomach a little bit." The CDC HSC awards points for encouraging the reporting of near misses, but multiple interviewees in this study stated that they have worked in places where reporting of injuries was frowned upon.

He continued by sharing another example of an employer where he had a near-injury miss. There was not a reportable injury, but the fear of what happened haunted him for the rest of his tenure at that company. He described the situation by saying that:

"I also had a big stack of vacuum cleaners tip over behind me. I heard it and I was able to get out of the way just in time."

"So, that was good, but every time I thought I was going to have something fall on me I'd move out real quick. I ended up hurting my back because I moved wrong. I had something heavy and I thought something was going to fall on top of me. I moved out of the way and then I hurt myself trying to not get hurt." Therefore, even a near miss is a reason to investigate the cause and create corrective measures.

The employee in a 500-person electrical company emphasized that occupational health and safety is a major part of their work on a day-to-day basis. He stated that "being in the construction industry, OSHA is big, and big for company insurance. Emergency response is probably the only unpreventable incident on a job site that somebody could do something about. Some of the CPR training is required by law or required by insurance. If somebody has an electric shock, you need to have someone trained in CPR because proper first aid and CPR could be the difference of life and death." Further research could investigate any instances where the other categories of the CDC HSC are required by law and if organizations pursue adherence with the same vigor that these companies pursue occupational health and safety.

An interviewee from organization with 125-employees in the technical services industry expressed how an injury in the company can really emphasize the importance of occupational health and safety. The engineer shared that "there was a guy that didn't work for (our company), but it was for the contractor in Chicago. It was his first day on-site, he was three stories up and they had a pit in the middle of the building. Instead of hooking here, then going, unhooking, coming back, unhooking, he unhooked here and went to walk across and fell and died." Of course this was a tragedy throughout the company, but it is also an ongoing expense, according to the interviewee. He explained that "now they're paying someone $130,000 to stand around. It's a safety officer. He sits up there for $130,000 a year. There's a bunch of safety stuff online that you had to do when you started." Further research could investigate the total cost of an injury in various industries and compare that to the cost of prevention in organizations that have not experienced deadly injuries.

"We have a profit sharing model based on workplace injuries that required outside medical treatment. If you got too many of those everyone lost out on the profit sharing; so hiding injuries was encouraged."

The last organization in the middle-scoring category provided an example of how a well-meaning policy can deter the accurate reporting of injuries in the area of occupational health and safety. The interviewee in this retail/wholesale trade industry stated that "they encouraged the reporting of injuries and they said that it was important to them that you reported it as soon as it happened. However, if you went to certain people they'd kind of be like, "Yes, why don't you keep working and see how it plans out by the end of the shift." Part of the problem, according to the employee in the study, was the "profit sharing model that they had with the employees. It was set up according to how many workplace injuries that required outside medical treatment. If you got too many of those everyone lost out on the profit sharing." Further research could investigate companies that did not tie injury reporting to profit sharing and how they performed in each of those metrics.

The organizations in the lowest-scoring category did more elaborating on the category of occupational health and safety than most of the other categories in the CDC HSC. An engineer in an automobile supplier with 450 employees stated that "our safety department is getting drilled right now, meaning it was lacking a lot. The first three to four months I worked there we didn't even have a health and safety manager. They recently hired her on, probably like six months ago, seven months ago. They're getting focused because they're getting audited."

He continued that, in his opinion, occupational health and safety was allowed to lack because their organization is not a union based company. In the interview, he shared that "he wouldn't say that they pride themselves on their workers and the only reason why I say no is because it's not a necessity. They don't need to do it. I know it sounds bad but when it comes down to it, it's more about the company's wellbeing than the workers. I mean, there is worker well-being but at the end of the day when you actually see the schedule and you see what's on it and it's designed to help the company, not the employee." Further research could investigate instances where companies put the employee first and yet still come out ahead in profitability versus companies that put the quarterly stock price first.

A family-owned automobile repair shop with seven employees does not have the resources of the bigger organizations in the study, but they still consider occupational health and safety to be an important part of their worksite. As the interviewee was quoted in an earlier section, an organization that only has seven employees cannot afford to miss anyone for very long. According to the interviewee, the owner assumes the responsibilities a safety manager would conduct at a larger organization. He stated that the owner "goes through the shop and if you're doing something (unsafe), he'll let you know. 'You ain't supposed to be doing it like that. What's wrong with you? What are you doing it like that for? You know better.'"

He continued by sharing more information on the company's overall culture toward health and safety. In his words, "everybody in the shop is kind of old school. If you cut your finger, whatever, it's put duct tape on it and go back to work. They just kind of work through it. If somebody cut their finger and they have duct tape on it, they ain't trying to hide. You know what I mean? It ain't like when Dad walks out they're putting it in their pocket or anything like that." New workers do receive on-the-job training about how to avoid injuries. They will shadow someone for a while, until they understand safe ways to perform in the shop.

"In order to be licensed, you're already expected to be trained in OSHA; if you don't have experience with that, then we don't need you."

The smallest organization in the study, a six-employee electrical service provider stated that knowledge of occupational health and safety is standard knowledge in their profession. The interviewee stated that "we don't have any written guidelines ourselves because, in our trade, in order to be licensed, you're already expected to be trained in OSHA. That's part of the job description. If you don't have experience with that, then we don't need you. Or you have an apprentice with you, and they are your responsibility, you train them on those types of guidelines."

PART 4: BEST PRACTICES, ANOMALIES, A MILLENIAL, FUTURE RESEARCH

16. SUMMARY OF BEST PRACTICES

HIGH-LEVERAGE WAYS TO INCREASE
HEALTH SCORE CARD POINTS

In this section, we will examine high-leverage ways to increase an organization's HSC score. By high-leverage, the author means efforts that leaders can exert that do not cost a lot in time or resources, yet still provide benefits (and points on the Health Score Card) in a number of categories. Many of the categories in the HSC award points to employers for education, classes, training, literature, live or through online portals for each of the categories. There are a number of free resources that employers can provide from community organizations, such as police, fire, and EMT professionals, the YMCA, local public health agencies, or even videos on YouTube from reputable health organizations. Additionally, 95% of the organizations in the study provide health insurance or connect employees to health insurance resources. Many of these health insurance providers offer information through online portals or in-person. By connecting employees to these resources once a year, the organization can earn several more points in nearly every category of the HSC.

SUMMARY OF BEST PRACTICES, ORGANIZED BY CATEGORY

This section provides a brief summary of the best practices in the various categories of the book so far. It is provided as a reference and review for the readers that want to work on one concept in a particular category, or multiple categories. The raised text on most pages along the way also attempted to provide a workable concept idea on each page. This section does the same, as a review. It is the author's hope that people will read these reminders and put the ideas into practice.

ORGANIZATIONAL SUPPORTS

The CDC HSC encourages employers to support their workforce in very broad, wide-reaching ways at the organizational and/or upper management level. The structure and policies of the organization can tell a lot about their commitment to health and wellness. Many of the highest-scoring organizations in this study use a health risk assessment. As previously mentioned, a study of wellness programs conducted by the school of Public Health at Harvard University, found that 80% of companies with wellness programs use the health risk assessment as the initial requirement in their wellness programs. (Baicker et al., 2010) Participation "is almost always voluntary" and selection bias can be a major problem in these types of programs, because the rest of the programs for all of the employees follow this initial information. (Baicker et al., 2010)

"The highest scoring organizations typically contract with local doctors to provide a health assessment at a clinic."

The organizations with the highest scores in this study showed a strong collaboration with medical professionals in their health assessments. Employers demonstrated commitment to their employees' health by using blood work to guide feedback from the assessments and providing one-on-one conversations during and after health assessments. The highest scoring organizations typically contract with local doctors to provide a health assessment at a clinic affiliated with their organization, or a health clinic in the community. A health clinic onsite that offered a variety of free programs was likely the role model of support in this study.

Wellness programs that provide rewards for completing a participatory health risk assessment are the most common type of wellness program in the United States. (Pomeranz, 2015) The incentives provided by these programs can raise concerns about their voluntary nature and the Americans with Disabilities Act of 1990 states that employers cannot require health-related inquiries and exams. (Pomeranz, 2015). Information gathered from a health risk assessment, such as weight, blood pressure, or blood lipid levels, or any other biometric data must be voluntary because it can determine health status, physical activity, or smoking activity. (Mello & Rosenthal, 2008) All of this data must be handled in compliance with HIPPA, the ADA, GINA, and be treated as confidential and separate from personnel records. (EEOC, 2011)

The top-scoring organizations in this study offered a variety of incentives for participation in their health and wellness programs. Multiple organizations offer cheaper insurance premiums for certifying as a non-smoker. Another company offers employees a 'non-wellness plan' and a 'wellness plan' to save 30% on insurance premiums. Others offer lower, but more frequent incentives, such as $10 for participating in wellness screenings, regular lunch and learns, and for watching health-related YouTube videos. Further, one company provides employees six hours of extra flex-time to use at the health center for check-ups, a health assessment, or anything relating to an illness.

"High-scoring organizations in this study provide a free gym membership and award prizes for the most gym attendance."

As stated previously, health assessments are almost voluntary, but employers are offering incentives directly for participating in the assessments. One high-scoring company offers an insurance discount for participating in a yearly health screening. Some companies pay employees cash to participate in yearly health assessments, while another gives employees with a family $1200 in their HSA account annually, $600 for employees without a family for participant in a health assessment. Other high-scoring organizations in this study provide a free gym membership and award prizes for the most gym attendance. Using the company-provided gym membership can earn points for each visit and these points can be traded for merchandise. Another company gives employees a bonus for using all their vacation time as more of a mental health initiative.

Providing flexible work hours can demonstrate organizational support and most of the best-scoring organizations had methods for providing flexible work environments for their employees. Perhaps the most unique program was the "school day program," that allows parents to match their children's' school schedule in the summer, on weekends, during the weekday, and even on inclement weather days. The corporate care manager of this organization felt that this was a very worthwhile program because good employees are hard to find in their area. He felt this was just one more barrier they could remove for segments of their workforce that allowed them to contribute to the company. Other high-scoring organizations have multiple schedules through the week and informal flexibility if employees have a need.

According to the CDC HSC, communication to employees through multiple channels is an important factor to encourage participation in wellness programs. According to a RAND wellness study in 2013, organizations should use multiple communication channels to inform employees of the services available. (Moseley & Estrada-Portales, 2013) Employers can use email, bulletin boards, announcements at company meetings, and health fairs to deliver clear messages about the goals and importance of wellness programs. (Moseley & Estrada-Portales, 2013) Effective wellness programs also allow input from employees, or two-way communication when developing clear goals and objectives. (Goetzel et al., 2014)

The highest-scoring organizations in the study demonstrated the types of communications mentioned in the studies above. They also seem to have a culture where an emphasis on health and wellness was embedded in formal and informal channels of communications. Examples of the best communication practices in this study include health communications being delivered personally by supervisors speaking to five to ten people, a 'brag wall' to spotlight healthy employees and spotlight success stories in their weekly or monthly newsletters, and increased annual health communications around the open enrollment period.

Other best practices in health and wellness communications include organizations that offering different activities to go along with each national health months, such February is Heart Month. One high-scoring organization used name brand health initiatives, for instance Acme-Gym, Acme-Kitchen, Acme-Garden and listing health in their organizational goals as one of five core company values. Employers in the study also held corporate health fairs, provide a fitness center in every location, grow vegetables in the corporate garden, and have a goal of providing health screenings for 90% of employees or more. Lastly, organizations that demonstrated an "extra-mile" level of support for health and wellness in their culture by paying 'very big' premiums each year to keep the insurance costs down for employees, providing volunteer time off for employees to participate in community events, and taking up donations to pay the expenses of a sick employee's above-insurance expenses.

TOBACCO CONTROL

"One of the highest scoring organizations in the study went to great lengths to celebrate successful cessation."

Organizations can demonstrate tobacco control by having written and posted policies that ban tobacco use on company property through multiple channels of communication. In a study in Washington State, researchers found that "few employers link smokers to evidence-based, cost-effective tobacco cessation practices." The study found that less than 6% of employers referred employees to the state-sponsored quit line. (Hughes et al., 2011) Therefore, it is not enough just to have a no tobacco policy but employers need to communicate through signs, employee meetings, corporate newsletter, and by not providing ashtrays. Organizations should also refrain from selling tobacco products on company property through vending machines, a snack bar, cafeteria, or gift shop.

Organizations in the study feel that sensitivity over tobacco control has increased over a short period of time. The highest-scoring organizations in this study are taking steps to improve tobacco control by reducing barriers to cessation counseling. One of the highest scoring organizations in the study went to great lengths to celebrate successful cessation and provide free resources for tobacco users. However, they still tobacco use as one of their biggest challenges. As stated previously in the paper, over 50% of employees under twenty-one admit to smoking.

NUTRITION

Organizations can earn points on the HSC by practicing nutrition in a number of ways. Sharing educational materials about nutrition, subsidizing healthier food, providing a food storage location and encouraging a nearby farmer's market are all activities that can earn points on the CDC HSC. The CDC HSC encourages written policies that provide healthier food and beverage choices in the company cafeteria, snack bar, and vending machines. Simple cost shifting that subsidizes healthier foods can reduce health care costs for the workforce. Organizations that offer less price reductions on lower-fat foods have shown higher sales on those items. (French, 2003)

The CDC HSC states that employee education can be another powerful tool for improving nutrition in the workplace. For instance, companies can provide health promotion materials on the benefits of proper nutrition. Organizations can also provide seminars, workshops, guidelines, or even self-management programs that help employees stay focused on their nutrition.

The very best practices in this study included active communication with vending companies to provide healthy options and a corporate garden onsite that provides salad materials for employees. One of the highest scoring companies provided a salad bar at the company cafeteria every day, which the employee attributed to dramatic weight loss during a short internship one summer.

"One remarkable program was the subsidized meal preparation, where for $150 a week, prepared meals are delivered to the employee's house."

The interviewee discussing this loved the program because of the health, ease, and convenience, but he also appreciated that the company would take the time to care enough to help them in this way.

In this study, organizations have seen an active shifting from unhealthy food to healthy options at meetings. Other highest scoring organizations will buy healthy food and beverages but not unhealthy food and beverages for employees. For instance, the company will give out water but charge for soda and/or a company will provide lunch for meetings and that is usually healthy.

A technology services company scored really well and obtained a lot of loyalty in the nutrition category by providing free, organic snacks from Whole Foods. Additionally, employees are allowed and encouraged to cook a healthy breakfast together. The giving away of fresh fruit and vegetables was a common theme throughout the study, whether it was from the corporate garden, employees with gardens, or just as a kind gesture. One interviewee felt that the only healthy nutrition the company stressed was staying hydrated. In the employee's opinion, this was seen as a negative, but it can also be seen as a vital part of nutrition in a hot warehouse where people were fainting on a weekly basis. Proper hydration can be a fundamental building block of nutrition and a great starting point for organizations that are just beginning a wellness program.

LACTATION SUPPORT

Lactation support, providing a private space, a breast pump, and flexible break times can demonstrate organizational support for nursing mothers. One of the most telling statistics in the literature review was from a study in 2004 concluded that there was a 94% return-to-work rate after maternity leave for women participating in an employer sponsored lactation program. (Ortiz et al., 2004)

The "extra-mile" level of action was demonstrated by a company that paid for breast milk to be shipped back home to an employee's baby while she was working out of town. Another organization incentivized participation by providing employees with a free breast pump if they participate in a prenatal program. More basic, but still important level of engagement, were shown by high-scoring organizations that gave all employees breaks that can be used for lactation support, providing a lactation room set aside with a breast pump, and offering maternity and paternity leave.

PHYSICAL ACTIVITY

"Group stretching time in the morning and in the afternoon helped employees move, take their mind off of their work, and prevented injuries."

The CDC HSC recognizes companies that provide an exercise facility on site, subsidizing or discounting the cost of an offsite facility, and providing environmental supports for physical activity. The Journal of Preventative Medicine suggests a combination of actions to encourage physical activity. (Sallis et al., 1998) For instance, a walking path is encouraged in a suburban location, while signage or a competition to promote using the stairs is effective in an urban setting. (Sallis et al., 1998) Step counting activities, such as tracking and friendly competitions, can change behaviors to encourage more activity, in part because it relies on data, rather than just self-reporting. (Slootmaker et al., 2009)

High-scoring organizations in this study employed a number of activities to increase movement amongst their employees. Group stretching time in the morning and in the afternoon helped employees move, take their mind off of their work, and prevented injuries. Another group included posters of all seven stretches that the employees conducted at the beginning of each day. The next-level of physical activity was demonstrated by an organization providing tai chi, yoga, and work station movement trainings on site.

"Social programs that encourage companionship can be an effective strategy for increasing physical activity in a population."

Social interaction around physical activity may be key to participation. Accessibility to bike paths, footpaths, health clubs, and swimming pools have been found to be associated with increased physical activity, but may be insufficient on their own. (Humpel, Owen, & Leslie, 2002) In the past, health professionals focused on previous habits that worked for their schedule in developing a physical activity wellness program (King, 1998). A 'social marketing strategy' that includes community-based surveys, feasibility studies, and focus groups can help to optimize the type, format, location, and date of the program is effective to encourage participation. (King, 1998) Additionally, social programs that encourage companionship and esteem support can be an effective strategy for increasing physical activity in a population. (Cavallo et al., 2012)

The higher-scoring organizations in the study offered a number of socially coordinated physical activities. Multiple organizations offered organized yoga and Pilates classes for stress reduction, physical movement, and social activity. Other organizations provided portable basketball goals, memberships at a gym within walking distance, and basketball as a group each week for employees. Other organizations use walking as a social, physical movement activity. In multiple organizations, there are walking routes around the lake and woods near the company's campus and employees form walking groups around a route called the "Mayor's Mile" in the industrial park. Further, one organization from the study teamed employees in "comrades" or buddies and encouraged or required them to walk together each week. This helped with physical activity as well as team-building and stress management, according to the interviewee.

WEIGHT MANAGEMENT

The highest-scoring organizations in this study used chaplains to address mental health as a root cause of over eating, individualized coaching sessions for employees, and confidential Employee Assistance Programs (EAPs). These interviewees discussed that the chaplain, the nurses, and other mental health professionals believe that

---

Over-eating is often the symptom of deeper emotional issues. The chaplain or counselor can help employees address the root cause of the over-eating.

The have a unique feature in that it is totally confidential and built on trust to encourage employees. Employees may obtain any service from the EAP, relating to emotional issues, overeating, drug use, etc. The EAP service will send a bill to the organization that does not even include the employee's name.

Other organizations use less intensive, yet still effective methods for helping employees with weight management. One high-scoring organization use BMI testing as part of an annual health assessment self-management program. Others use BMI testing at any time of the year, and the company will pay for 50% of Body Mass Index (BMI) testing if the employee will match the other 50%. A number of employers in the study use Weight Watchers at their facility or in the community, depending on the number of interested employees. January was repeatedly mentioned as a prime month for starting a Weight Watchers or gym-based programs for employees.

STRESS MANAGEMENT

The highest-scoring organizations in this study engaged in a number of the activities mentioned in the preceding paragraph. For instance, employers consistently mentioned that they provide dedicated stress-free zones, such as fitness rooms or break rooms, "phone booths" that are available throughout the office where employees can have privacy, and temporary stress free zones. One employer dedicates a conference room to an employee-ran bible study and related activities during the lunch hour and break times, as well as lunch time yoga. As one might expect, holiday parties and team-building events on and offsite were very popular in this study. One organization, based on employee feedback, has begun providing resources for employees with PTSD onsite.

Participants in a workplace study on online support and stress management found that "the percentage of participants who reported practicing meditation at least once per week was greater among those with group support than without group support; 94% versus 54%." (Allexandre et al., 2016) Employees also benefit by being included in the decision-making process for issues that impact job stress. Stress related issues can include changes in work schedules, time management demands, specific work practices, and work processes.

Morning meetings can allow employees to provide feedback and suggest improvements regarding the previous day and for the upcoming day and week.

Some organizations provide counselors or HR members to whom employees can speak to about workplace issues. In the construction industry, it was common that employees can take off when they want to, they just do not get paid for it. This allows them to more easily navigate issues in their person lives, if they can afford to miss work. This individual also stated that stress is more prevalent when there is no work for days than when one is actually busy. Employers can take care to ensure that employees do not suffer from boredom for prolonged periods. This employee left his previous employer because his work was very boring. He even found that the boredom bled into his personal life and he found himself just laying around the house on the weekends and other times he was off from work.

One middle-scoring organization cited tension between production employees and non-production employees. He mentioned that a lot of the tension is related to unclear expectations and misunderstandings from each of what the other group is doing or supposed to be doing. In his interview, he felt that 95% of people were complaining about something. If there were formal mechanisms for communicating about these feelings before the tensions escalated, it could likely help reduce the amount of tension.

DEPRESSION

"Depression can be difficult to diagnose because employees will avoid diagnosis because of stigma, denial, or lack of knowledge."

Depression was a category that did not receive as much attention as the other categories, even if organizations did enough "in the last twelve months" to obtain a high score on the HSC. Employees suffering from depression can impact the organization through loss of productivity, absenteeism, and other hard to quantify ways. The World Health Organization (WHO) ranks depression (major depressive disorder (MDD)) as the "fourth leading cause of disability worldwide." (Murray & Lopez, 1996) Employers in this study, most often left the reporting of depression up to the employee; whereas physical activity, tobacco control, and even stress management had specific programs to treat those issues.

Organizations in this study demonstrated multiple times that the treating and screening of depression was the responsibility of the employee. For instance, a high-scoring company on the HSC overall stated that "the EAP information on depression is posted on the bulletin board." Other organizations stated that depression is not discussed openly, employees have to ask for the resources, and that the culture is such that employees need to fix their own depression problems. Other organizations have hotlines for drug use and depression that employees can call and pamphlets on depression that employees can have, when they ask for them.

Depression can be difficult to diagnose for a number of reasons. Employees can avoid diagnosis because of stigma, denial, lack of physician skill or knowledge, "lack of availability of providers and treatments, limitations of third-party coverage, and restrictions on specialist, drug, and psychotherapeutic care." (Goldman et al., 1999) Past research has underestimated the link between burnout and depression. Treatments for depression may help workers identified as burned out, due to the overlap. (Schonfeld & Bianchi, 2016) The CDC HSC provides credit whether the counseling is provided in-house, provided by an outside vendor, or offered through a health insurance program. Workplaces are also encouraged to train their managers on how to "recognize depression, productivity or safety issues, and (provide) company or community resources for managing depression." (CDC, 2014)

Organizations in this study encourage employees to see the chaplain for depression and other emotional issues. One of the highest-scoring and progressive organizations in this study had an interesting approach in treating and providing resources for depression. While they offer free resources for almost every other category in the CDC HSC, they ask employees to pay something for depression services. Of course, they will help employees that cannot afford the services, but they want employees to have "skin in the game" when it comes to depression treatment. This was an interesting distinction because they spend a lot of money on all kinds of wellness resources other than depression.

Other high-scoring organizations focus on depression in various ways. A very small manufacturer has a quarterly health review with a nurse and depression is a checkbox on that quarterly health review. Another interviewee stated that their small culture is closely intertwined and knowledge about one another. She stated that when employees are dealing with struggles in their personal lives, they all get together and help each other in a support group fashion. Another interviewee shared that any time there is an issue, everyone stops and takes care of the person who is struggling. This type of culture is very supportive if it already exists, but many organizations in the middle and low scoring categories have cultures where the wellness departments and individuals are separated.

Depression and especially employee burnout is perhaps the area where the most improvement can be made by organizations in this study.

HIGH BLOOD PRESSURE, HIGH CHOLESTEROL, AND DIABETES

Chronic diseases are the next categories addressed by the HSC. Similar to the other interventions discussed; high blood pressure, high cholesterol, and diabetes receive attention on the CDC HSC. Workplace wellness programs often have goals of achieving positive changes in employees' body mass, blood pressure, cholesterol, triglycerides, and glucose levels. (Hyatt Neville et al., 2011) Improvements in these levels can positively influence health care costs, productivity, long-term health, job satisfaction, absenteeism, long-term health and a sense of community. (Merrill et al., 2011)

The organizations in this study provide long-term treatment and education to help employees with chronic conditions. Their methods ranged from using biometric weight loss initiatives to address high blood pressure to focusing on the high cost of bad habits in educating employees. For instance, one company worked to educate employees on the daily cost of cigarettes and monster drinks.

The interviewees cited an instance where several of their employees were spending $15-$20 per day on monster and other energy drinks.

Another organization has a four-month long wellness program that deals with stress and high blood pressure issues. This length of program helps drive positive behavior change, according to the employee. Some organizations also have hospitals and primary care facilities that are affiliated with the organization; either as part of another facet of the organization or even wholly owned by the organization.

RESPONSE TO HEART ATTACK AND STROKE

The CDC HSC encourages participants to receive training and be aware of the signs and symptoms of heart attack and stroke. This includes posters or flyers in common areas that convey heart attacks and strokes are as emergencies. The CDC HSC awards points if there is an adequate number of AEDs such that any person can reach an AED within three to five minutes of an emergency. Organizations are encouraged to communicate their emergency response plans to local first responders, notifying them of the plan that is in place.

The high-scoring organizations in this study had many of the characteristics described by the CDC HSC. Multiple organizations stated that they have a standing committee for emergency response; that the entire HR team was required to be CPR and First Aid certified, and that many employees on the floor are also EMTs in the community. The local chamber of commerce, the American Heart Association, and local fire-fighters offer free CPR, AED, basic first aid classes; therefore many middle and lower scoring organizations in this study and in the community have access to these resources if they wish.

The highest scoring organizations have emergency response teams in place that conduct intermittent training with CPR and defibrillators throughout the year. A high-scoring, but small organization provides all twenty-five employees went through CPR training that was paid for by the company. A large manufacturer touted several trained first responders on staff that all carry radios and a medical kit. Many organizations in the high and medium categories stated that everyone in management, from supervisor and up have emergency response training and there is always some trained in CPR at the facility.

Organizations in the study work on communication around emergency response. One very high-scoring organization awards the 'Save Award' when someone uses CPR on the job to save someone's life. Although it does not happen very often, they felt it was important to make a very big deal out of an incident like this, because it keeps everyone focused on the tools they have to save lives. Other organizations encourage a lot of dialog on safety and security. One employer with a lot of Muslim employees stated that employees faint more often during Ramadan. Therefore, they have increased emergency response efforts at this time of the year.

OCCUPATIONAL HEALTH AND SAFETY

The organizations in this study had a strong focus on occupational health and safety. The high-scoring organizations mentioned that they have several occupational nurses as every facility, they use industry standards to guide safety programs, and at every facility, every day there are emergency response teams on staff. They also have policies to never blame the associate for an injury and the active use of a safety committee on a weekly or monthly basis. One social services organization stated that their funding is tied to certain levels of government and they require safety standards that must be met.

A trend amongst more office-related organizations was to ignore or have less of a focus on occupational health and safety. Some felt that it was not a priority because

"OSHA is not really required in an office setting."

Or that they are too small for OSHA to be required or that they do not have the financial resources to do more than the bare minimum for safety. However, there were organizations in the office setting that provide standing desks and headphones for telephone usage to reduce or prevent repetitive motion injuries. Another very-small, 25-employee organization uses part-time traveling nurses that go from company to company in order to provide an occupational nurse without the cost of a full-time nurse employee. Another organization provides high quality footwear for employees that are on their feet all day. This may seem like a small expense, at approximately $200 per year per employee, but the interviewee that mentioned it beamed with pride that his organization cared so much about his daily needs.

COMMUNITY COALITION OPPORTUNITIES

As the research was being compiled, multiple community coalition opportunities emerged. First of all, the seventeen of the twenty of the organizations in the study were less than a thirty minute drive from one another. Clusters of organizations were less than ten minutes from one another. Furthermore, multiple organizations are located in industrial parks within walking distance of one another and many other similar organizations. The author is a member of the local chamber of commerce and their health and wellness coalition. The organizations in this study and these industrial parks are members of this chamber and other chambers of commerce that are continually seeking ways to provide value to their members.

Many natural areas of community health and wellness synergy became apparent when analyzing these seemingly isolated organizations.

First of all, four different organizations within walking distance mentioned health and/or safety fairs. One organization even mentioned letting this offering "slide" because it was too much work. If these organizations can work together to provide one health and safety fair for themselves and their industrial park, perhaps it can have a bigger impact. The same logic of community collaboration applies to educational seminars and communication resources for each of the HSC categories. Finally, three of the four highest scoring organizations and two other organizations are within walking distance of a large and free community exercise facility.

One of these organizations even mentioned that they could not provide an on-site facility to their employees because there was not enough interest for an on-site facility. A follow-up call was made to the manufacturing manager to inform him of the free community facility within walking distance and he was previously unaware of the facility.

17. ANOMALIES IN FINDINGS

The first anomaly that will be discussed in the findings was that an automobile supplier in the manufacturing industry scored nearly perfectly on the CDC HSC, but they still mentioned several instances of having a culture of unhealthy behavior. In the interviews with this organization, the three interviewees were very excited about the many health initiatives offered at their organization. As the table above demonstrates, they scored a 261 out of a possible 264 points. The only question they missed on the CDC HSC was that they did not offer 50% or more healthy versus non-healthy food in their vending machines, cafeterias, food trucks, etc. They have even tried to offer more than 50% in the past, but they found that sales for the vending companies plummet and they have to go back to less than 50% of healthy food offerings.

In spite of all of these health and wellness resources, the interviewees mentioned many health issues that plague their workforce. They stated that over 50% of their employees under 21 admitted to smoking. They are "plagued" with obesity and related chronic diseases, and weight management is one of their most serious challenges. They also mentioned that many of their employees who travel on the road will drink four to five Monster energy drinks a day or an equivalent amount of soda and sugary soft drinks. The reason this organization is mentioned in the anomaly section is that it causes one to ask the questions:

- If an organization with all of these resources and a strong history of wellness still has a very unhealthy workforce, how can smaller companies with less resources hope to have a healthy workforce?

- If this organization scored so high on the CDC HSC, but has a very unhealthy workforce, is the CDC HSC a good indicator of healthy employees or just healthy activities?

Perhaps future research can help answer these questions and determine how to help organizations with this same demographic to create a health workforce.

A LOT OF RESOURCES DOES NOT MEAN A HIGH WELLNESS SCORE

The second anomaly to discuss in this section involves a very large organization with, presumably, a lot of resources who did not score very well on the HSC. In this study, a retail/wholesale trade organization was the largest company in the study but in the bottom third of scores.

This organization scored a 101 out of a possible 264 on the HSC. This score was in the bottom third of our study, well below the average score for the study, and even further below the average score from the CDC Validation Study. There were a two categories where they scored markedly higher than the CDC Study, and these were emergency response to heart attack and stroke and occupational health and safety. In this industry, for this size of company (2500 employees), these areas are required and monitored closely by law and government agencies.

This organization and their scores are high-lighted because many of the smaller organizations felt that they did not provide these resources because they were too small and did not have the money to provide health and wellness programs. It is worth pointing out that a working at a very large organization is no guarantee of many offerings of health and wellness programs. One explanation can be that this organization is in a very competitive industry and they are continually lowering costs internally and prices externally for the customer. The competitive nature of their industry might be an explanation for their lack of health and wellness offerings.

ONE VERY SMALL COMPANY RECEIVED A VERY HIGH SCORE

The third anomaly to discuss in this section is a contrasting example to the organization above. The study included a very small manufacturer, with

25 employees, scored 237 out of 264 on the CDC HSC. This organization offered a multitude of health and wellness programs for their employees and was the third highest-scoring organization in the study. They offered yoga and Pilates classes twice a week, had a quarterly checkup and evaluation with a nurse (followed by one-on-one counseling if desired), and they provided subsidized meal-preparation for all employees each week for the employees. This organization also offered in-depth safety training each month, CPR and AED training to all employees, and the highest available lactation support according to the CDC HSC.

Other organizations in the study, large and small, may be wondering how this employer can provide so many offerings with only 25 employees. This study did not focus on that question, but the researcher will speculate now to offer ideas for future research. Perhaps their very small organization is the reason why they could offer so many health and wellness activities. Additionally, they operate in a health and wellness industry, so the owner and the employees may be drawn to these programs by their very nature as individuals. Further, they might have a very high-profit and/or high-margin product that provides the resources for these programs.

A VERY HEALTHY AND PROGRESSIVE COMPANY SCORED IN THE MIDDLE OF THE STUDY

The fourth anomaly to discuss in this section is that of an organization that exhibits many very healthy behaviors, but then ends up in the middle-scoring category. This organization is a 3-D design company that is very healthy but did not have initiatives relating to chronic diseases or emergency response to heart attack and stroke.

This organization scored very well on the first seven categories of the HSC, but then failed to score above average in categories relating to chronic disease or on issues relating to heart attack and stroke. Part of the reason for this lack of focus could be that they are an office environment, so they are not required to have CPR, AED, or first aid training like many of the manufacturers claimed. Additionally, this interviewee stated that everyone, including the owners, were less than 35 years of age, so chronic disease or heart attack and stroke were not relevant to their work force, in her words.

19. A MILLENNIAL'S PERSPECTIVE ON HEALTH: A SOLE PROPRIETOR FOCUSES ON WORKPLACE WELLNESS

"We feel insurance is a scam that we are forced into. I'll just pay the fines and not have health insurance."

This case study of a sole proprietorship is included at the end of the chapter to share the thoughts of a mid-20s entrepreneur in the technology industry. He faces different challenges in the same health and wellness categories as the larger organizations in this study. His perspective provides insight into, not only the challenges a one-person company faces with health and wellness, but also the attitude of a millennial toward the health and wellness industry.

This section will share the sole-proprietor's opinions on the health system and how he addresses his health and wellness challenges without health insurance or an organization to provide resources for his health and wellness. The over-riding feeling this interviewee had toward the health industry is that it was not a good value for his money. For instance, if he were to obtain health insurance, it would cost him $100-$200 per month and then he would have a $5,000 premium to use his benefits in the event he needed them. In his words, "we (he and his wife) felt it was a scam that we were forced into paying for this, and then if we don't buy it, we get the tax fees. I'll just pay the fines and not have health insurance. Whenever something did go wrong, we looked it up online, we'd find the solution. I didn't have any major issues, so I was perfectly fine. There are a handful of places (to obtain healthcare) in the city that do accept cash, and the cash discounts are huge. You actually end up saving money by going and paying cash at places."

He also feels that, in the event of catastrophic health care needs, he can take advantage of Personal Injury Protection, or PIP, in Kentucky. His understanding is that "if you get into a car accident, you are entitled to like $10,000 of healthcare, basically. That money can go towards chiropractor, massage, just injury done to you by vehicles when you're in a car. It's still insurance. It's still the same. It's funded by Kentucky, so the state is kinda protecting people to some degree." He is aware that there is a penalty for not having insurance and he described this situation.

"I feel like insurance companies are just screwing everyone right now. Their cheapest packages are a flat out joke and they're still triple the price that I'd be willing to pay."

He described his experience with the penalty by stating that "the first year, I didn't get charged somehow. The next time, it was like $1200 or something. This year, it's like $2,000. They keep making it bigger, the penalty, as (President Obama) left. With the change of presidency, they're trying to undo that so that penalty is gonna change again and be lessened." From his viewpoint, this penalty is less than the $100-$200 a month for insurance, combined with the $5,000 deductible. He stated that "'You know what? Screw it. Okay. We'll see what happens. Kinda roll the dice. I hope that as I get older, new options are available, different options, and I'll address it as it goes. As of right now, I think it's a joke."

He continued sharing his feelings about health insurance and his perceived lack of value. In his opinion, he said that "I feel like they're just screwing everyone right now. Their cheapest packages are a flat out joke and they're still triple the price that I'd be willing to pay. The fact that I can get the Adobe software suite for $50 a month, thousands and thousands of dollars of software, value added, something I can actually make money with, that's value. That's value to me. For them to say, 'For $110 a month, you're still gonna be paying deductibles. You have to pay another $5,000 before you can see a penny from us,' I'm sorry, that's not value. That's just bad business and they can get away with it because everyone's forced to purchase it. It's a monopoly. They can all raise their rates. In his opinion, if the bottom plan was $10, $25 a month, it would be worth it for him to purchase the plan. But, he continued that "at $110 (a month) with no value added, I think it's a form of theft in its current state. If there was a $1,000 deductible and $25 a month plan, I'd make some effort to sign up for that."

This interviewee also described his feelings toward insurance companies and experiences he has had with them in the past. His wife is a small-business owner and a health care provider, and they deal with insurance companies regularly as part of her business. He stated that "I should say, we have to deal with insurance companies a lot. They're thugs. They are absolute punks. What happens is she'll send an invoice for $1200 because she rendered $1200 worth of service. Then they'll say, 'Oh, well we don't have your money right now. We'll give you $600 and we'll write the check today.' She's like, 'No, the invoice is for $1200. We rendered that much service.' They're like, 'Okay, well it's gonna be two weeks before we get that check out to you.' She's like, 'No.' Then they will say, 'Okay, would you take $800 for a check today?' They play these games to try to get you. They start like 50%. They start halfway and try to trick you into saying yes and then they can pay you less and then give you your money. We just say, 'no, we'll just take the full price in two weeks. Thank you.'" His feeling of insurance not being a sound financial value, coupled with negative experiences that created a feeling of contempt combine to create a desire to avoid doing business with health insurance companies.

"I got a cold. I had infected sinus, but I looked on YouTube. I was like, 'infected sinus, what do I do?' Get all these things to treat it. It got better."

The sole-proprietor does use healthcare and has the occasional bought with bad health. In the interview, he described a situation of obtaining medication. In his words, "I'm prescribed to Adderall, so I had to go to refill my subscription. I had to re-up my prescription. It was like $95 to see the doctor, check my heart rate, make sure I'm still healthy enough to take my medicine, and then he wrote me a prescription and good to go." He also described a situation of treating himself through a cold and sinus infection He stated that "I got a cold. I had infected sinus, but I looked on YouTube. I was like, 'infected sinus, what do I do?' Get all these things to treat it. It got better. The primary care, the general physicians, they're not gonna die off, but the need for them has shrunk. Back when I was a kid, they had a monopoly on information. My mom, if she wanted to know what we needed to do to make me better, we had to go visit the doctor and they'd be like, 'Oh, let him rest and have some Tylenol and we'll bill your insurance company for you. Don't worry.' Today, the interviewee feels that the information is readily available to him, through personal contacts and the worldwide web.

The sole-proprietor does see the vulnerability in his situation and he discussed it in the interview. He described this vulnerability by stating that a major health catastrophe "is the only thing that scares me; serious health risks. Because then what happens, I don't know how that works. The government claims they still have to serve you, so if I did go into the ER with a broken arm, I think they would still help me. That's my biggest vulnerability right now. As far as just day to day living, small illnesses, small issues, the average person can fix a lot of those on their own now, I think. Just at their home and with some due diligence.

"It's not the safest. It's definitely much more like a wild west cowboy approach to healthcare, but that's just kinda how I am."

This interviewee shared an experience he had with the healthcare system in Belize and compared it to his experiences with the healthcare system in the United States. He used this story to help explain his feelings toward the U.S. healthcare system and why he does not feel it provides a worthwhile value. He described the experience in this way:

"We were in Belize last year, and this is when I saw just how horrible our system is. I was a visitor. Obviously I don't live there. I don't have anything but a passport. (Our friend) was so violently ill, she was puking all night because she got water poisoning. She started getting into fever and losing vision a little bit because of dehydration. We needed to get an IV in this girl. We gotta go to a hospital. All right, we're going to a hospital in Belize. Let's see what happens.

"What are we gonna owe for this hospital visit?'
They were even using materials. They used an IV bag
on her. 'No, it's free,' the doctor says."

"Belize amazing experience. We get there, and it's a little rundown building. The floors are a little dirty, but there's no wait. We walk in. A nurse doesn't greet you or a receptionist. It's the doctor. 'Hi. What's wrong?' Here's what's going on. She's like, 'Okay.' I was expecting her to say sit down or here's some paperwork. She's like, "Let's go on back." It was literally five seconds that we're sitting in the lobby just before she even walked up to us. We had a conversation, told her what was up. She took her back to the room, worked on her, gave her an IV. Probably 30, 45 minutes back there. I was just sitting in the waiting room waiting for (our friend) to come out and she comes out.

"I ask, 'What do we owe?' We were sitting there like, 'Okay, are we gonna owe $500, $1,000? What are we gonna owe for this hospital visit?' They were even using materials. They used an IV bag on her. 'No, it's free,' the doctor says. Then, I was like, 'okay, I gotta fill out a bunch of paperwork, you gotta see my visa numbers, I gotta prove that I'm a citizen of the US visiting this country.' They're like, 'No, oh no, no no. You walk in, we work on you, and you leave. The government just makes sure that this building's run and my salary's paid and that's it. That's all there is too it.' It's so simple. It was so clean. In and out.

We were back to our hotel. Perfectly fine. That's when I realized just how bad this system is and how big of a joke it was that in a third world country, middle of nowhere, we got a perfectly functioning hospital with no wait, no fees, no paperwork. Done. When I saw that, I was like, yeah, I'm not giving money to the U.S. system. I'm not gonna pay for insurance because if everyone does it, it's accepting that this works. It's everyone laying down like a dog and taking it. If no one does it, the insurance company's like, 'Okay, this isn't working. People still aren't buying it. They're just paying the fees to the government, not paying us. We gotta do something different here, guys.'

---

*"I make bad health choices. I know I'm making them,
I just haven't gotten past it yet. It's not that I don't
know how to prevent diabetes."*

The interview also discussed ways he addresses and does not address more long-term health concerns. He shared his views on health issues where one does not see the negative side effects for twenty years or more, such as stress management, diabetes, high cholesterol, high blood pressure, or obesity. He stated that those conditions are "a slow build." He stated that he is already starting to see negative side effects from his lifestyle. In his words, "I'm gaining weight. I got a bigger gut. You don't need to pay someone health insurance to learn how to take care of yourself. Again, I bounce back to YouTube. I know how to be healthy, but I make bad health choices. I know I'm making them, and I've tried to make changes, but because of these habits that I've built up, I just haven't gotten past it yet. It's not that I don't know how to prevent diabetes." This viewpoint seems to echo some of the highest scoring organizations in the study. They provide a lot of resources and incentives to drive good health, but the employees still choose to smoke, eat poorly, or live a sedentary lifestyle.

During the interview, this individual was asked to compare and contrast his experience as a sole-proprietor with other companies where he worked and with organizations where his friends currently work. He began by sharing how his situation can be worse off than individuals who work in a medium to large organization that provides health resources for their employees. He said that first, "I'll start with worse off. Because of these big groups of people, and especially my friends that all have little step trackers on them, they get discounts at work. That group mentality creates an accountability system. Just like we have mastermind groups for creating accountability, you have a whole work group of people like, 'Oh, I got 10,000 steps today.' Everyone's got 10,000 steps and high fiving each other and there's one guy that didn't. He's like, 'Damn, I'm out of the group.'" The interviewee felt that this comradery and accountability would help him with areas of health where he might not be excelling on his own. At the same time, he feels that a lot people in these corporate cultures may decide to do their own thing anyway and ignore the incentives and resources provided by their organizations.

"Others are sharing diseases with 300 people; all standing in the same elevators, pushing the same bathroom doors open."

In comparison to his friends that work at large organizations, he feels as though there are several areas where he has a better situation, for his health needs, than the people he knows with all of the resources. One example of a healthier situation, in his opinion, is that he is not sharing germs with a large community of people. In his words, "they're sharing diseases and issues with 300 people; all standing in the same elevators, pushing the same bathroom doors open. I'm in my own house by myself, 90% of my work life. I'm in my family room. I'm not exposed to many culture colds, or not so much. Other peoples' germs are one thing I'm not in contact with, which I think is probably a good thing. I'm probably a little healthier because I am not in a giant mega city of people every single day or in a parking lot."

He continued by sharing his feelings toward mental health and stress management. He believes that his position as a sole proprietor allows his to have less stress than the majority of people in larger organizations that have stress given to them by their bosses. As far as mental health goes, I couldn't have a better situation. He explained that "If I want to take a vacation tomorrow, I can leave the country for a month. My office isn't a physical location. It's a digital location. Everything I need, as long as I have the Internet, I can work. I can serve my clients. I can make money. I don't have to answer to anyone; I get to choose what kind of work environment I'm in."

The sole proprietor enjoys that he gets to choose the amount of hours he works at a time, the time of day he works, (which he loves to work at night) and if he wants to stand up or sit down. He also says that "I can take as long of breaks as I want. I also have the benefit of being in my own environment. I'm not stuck in a cube or in a office. I create my office. Obviously, you've seen I've spent a lot of time on my house, and it's because that's where I live and work. It's my cubicle. It's my backyard."

*"I'm able to stop while I'm working, walk outside,
and work on my waterfall for 30 minutes then go
back to work, it's huge."*

He also explained that he saves a lot of time and stress by not commuting into a work place. He stated that he saves a lot of time each day and he is able to choose a tone, or feeling, to start his day, other than a commute through rush hour traffic. In his words, "I save all that time by not being stuck in traffic. You start your day stuck in traffic, that's gonna start your day off on a stressful day and it's gonna start that foot off wrong. I wake up to two border collies rolling all over me and I go for a walk in my backyard, and then I open my computer and I work. That's about the most peaceful way to start a work day I could possible imagine, because that's the one I did imagine for myself." Perhaps other organizations could examine ways to allow their employees the ability to create a peaceful way to start and carry through their days, as this interviewee has done for himself. He also stated that "I didn't really consider that a part of my healthcare, but being able to stop while I'm working, walk outside, and work on my waterfall for 30 minutes then go back to work, it's huge. Most people's break is going outside to smoke a cigarette."

This interviewee also shared that his coworkers are not dictated to him by a manager and he feels that this eliminates a lot of stress that he had in the corporate world. In his words:

"When I was at a large organization, I was on a team of six people. One of them was a girlfriend. Obviously, I really liked her. The other one was this guy that I just butted heads with. He was my cubemate, so I was stuck every day with him and we were just constantly at odds. We're just very different people, but we aren't the boss. We don't get to pick who we work with, so you're stuck doing projects with this other person that you clash with, and that's a lot of mental stress. Also, I think it holds you back too because you can't do your best work, and then causes even more stress because of that.

"As far as stress and quality of life, that's where I'm at a pinnacle. Compared to I don't care who you're talking to. As far as I'm concerned, I've created the best life I can picture for myself. I have as close to zero stress world as possible.

"That doesn't mean that hackers won't come and knock down my server at some point and I gotta put it back up, and that week is stressful. Sometimes, shit happens. That's just life. Elements I control, I have a zero stress in the workplace. As far as health goes, especially in Eastern culture where they say the mind is really forming the body, I think that my body's at more peace and I'm healthier because my mind is always in such a great place, so that's a huge benefit."

Finally, the sole proprietor discussed the topic of nutrition. He feels as though he is at an advantage in his isolated situation because he is not subjected to "pitch-ins" of unhealthy food or vending machines that offer food he would not normally eat. He described a larger organization by stating that "every day, you walk in the lobby, there's that soda machine. You walk up to the break room, and then there are all kinds of sweet treats lying out. Then, if you were in that environment, you're probably a part of that peer pressure. If you're not pitching in on the cakes, you're not in that circle, then you feel like you're ousted from the community. They're also building more team and camaraderie, and you're the outlier and now you're sad because you're not part of the team." He felt that tobacco use was similar to low-nutrition food, because he was not subjected to peer pressure around tobacco or second-hand smoke.

This case study only looks at one individual, in one industry, the technical services industry. In spite of the limitation of a population size of one, this interview may shed some light on the feelings of millennials toward the health insurance industry, the U.S. healthcare system, and the modern workplace in general. It seemed important to include at least one entrepreneur, because there are a number of students that graduate from Purdue Polytechnic New Albany each year that choose to be own their own business at a large or small scale.

20. SUGGESTIONS FOR FUTURE RESEARCH

The research conducted in this study created more questions than answers for the researcher. This section will discuss a few of the suggestions for future research that emerged during the study. An organization from the pilot study stopped doing weight loss competitions because they began monitoring the blood work of participants in these challenges. They found that employees' bloodwork showed poor health outcomes because employees were "bulking up" before the challenge and then engaging in crash diets to lose as much weight, as fast as possible, to win the competition.

To learn more about the overall effectiveness of weight loss competitions, further research could compare the blood work amongst employees at all organizations, but that data is not available.

Another possibility for future research is the topic of investing in health programs in spite of employees eventually leaving the company. One interviewee stated that the thinking might change if leadership "could see that (health and wellness) is an investment, instead of a cost... you have to pay for it today, but you don't always see the benefit. And you may never be able to put a number on it." Future research could look at the return on investment of health programs, particularly if employee turnover negates the investments into health when employees leave the company.

Other organizations in the high-scoring category also use mass communications to share health information. The interviewee from the educational services industry indicated that their wellness communication is "pretty much generalized. There's general e-mail sent out at least monthly on wellness program and there's also flyers, so it's pretty much kind of a mass email." The CDC does not necessarily reward a more intimate and customized approach for communicating, but further research could investigate if it should change this approach.

A middle-scoring organization in the construction industry shared a unique approach to demonstrating top-down leadership commitment to health and wellness. Because all of their employees belong to an employee union, the union takes care of all of the wellness programs for employees. The supervisor explained that "all health programs are union driven. I don't think that they would provide anything if it wasn't for the union." Interestingly, the interviewee stated that employees get to vote on how to allocate any pay increases they receive. In his words, "the company pays our insurance. We have a package and if we get a raise, it's up to us to decide where the raise goes; whether to the benefits or on the check." Further research could solely investigate union-based organizations to see how these companies were involved in wellness, in addition to union efforts. The study could then compare the health outcomes and see if it is worthwhile for the organization to add programs beyond the union's programs.

"Do organizations that offer wellness programs experience less employee turnover than companies that do not invest in wellness?"

The engineer at an automobile supplier feels that there is a culture of caring and concern for all of the employees. In his words, "there are a lot of large companies that people feel like (they) just show up and push the button. They feel as though there are a million people that want to take my spot and I'm expendable." They interviewee feels that his company "doesn't look at their people like they're expendable and there's a lot of long term employees there. And I think it's because of the safety stuff, and the promoting the wellness." This statement could be explored in further research to see if these organizations experience less employee turnover than companies that do not invest in these programs.

An interviewee from a young company felt that the age of the employees affected the culture and the company's approach to health and wellness. He stated that "with everybody being so young, I wonder if there's no need to have a weight loss program and things like that. Further research can study the changes at this company throughout the years when everybody gets older and employees become more diverse in age and how they will adapt to that in health programs. Additionally, a manufacturing enterprise with 160-employees, stated that they do not focus on emergency preparedness. The interviewee, a young designer in his early twenties, stated that "I don't think there's really that need for that ... just looking at the employees that work there, we're all fairly young so it's never come up... it'd be kind of weird for them to give us a talk about heart ... is it heart disease or heart failure?" Further research could specifically investigate age-related issues and emergency response plans in organizations.

Are tobacco cessation programs and stress management programs counter to one another?

An organization in the technical services industry had evidence of heavy tobacco use in their culture. The interviewee, a non-smoker, had some strong feelings on the topic in the interview. He felt that "I think they know if they tried to get people to quit (tobacco) while they're on the road, they'd probably kill somebody. They have enough stress going on without having to make them do that. Tobacco control and stress management would basically be conflicted, (because) tobacco is their stress management. They just let people deal with stress in their own ways. For most of them, it's through smoking." Further research could investigate the possibility of offering both tobacco cessation and stress management to employees to see if they are indeed mutually exclusive as this interviewee stated.

Another company has walking groups that are not discouraged; however they are not an official company program. The organization from the transportation industry has an official walking route around the facility, directly across the street. The interviewee did not say it was provided by the company, but it is in a business park where many companies can access it. According to the interviewee, "it's called "The Mayor's Mile" or "Miracle Mile" or something like that." Further research might explore how local elected officials can endorse the built-environment to encourage physical activity.

One interviewee stated that people have had heart attacks in the plant. He continued by stating that "my uncle's dad had a heart attack and died. They went back on the videos and he was moving his arm all day and he had complained about it. He had called his wife and said he wasn't feeling good, sick to his stomach, and he was going to come home and lay down. He eventually crashed and burned in the back. Someone found him like 8 minutes later." Further research could investigate if employees, their family members, or their coworkers would take a different course of action when the signs and symptoms of heart attacks and strokes are widely and regularly discussed, coupled with a plan of action.

APPENDIX 1: THE CDC WORKSITE HEALTH SCORE CARD

An Assessment Tool to Prevent Heart Disease, Stroke, and Related Conditions Worksheet

Organizational Supports

During the past 12 months, did your worksite:

1. Conduct an employee needs and interests assessment for planning health promotion activities?

Answer "yes" if, for example, your organization administers focus groups or employee satisfaction surveys to assess your employee health promotion program(s).

Answer "no" if your organization administers general surveys that do not assess your employee health promotion program(s). (1 pt.) or (0 pts.)

2. Conduct employee health risk appraisals/assessments through vendors, on-site staff, or health plans and provide individual feedback plus health education?

Answer "yes" if, for example, your organization provides individual feedback through written reports, letters, or one-on-one counseling. (3 pts.) or (0 pts.)

3. Demonstrate organizational commitment and support of worksite health promotion at all levels of management?

Answer "yes" if, for example, all levels of management participate in activities, communications are sent to employees from senior leaders, the worksite supports performance objectives related to healthy workforce, or program ownership is shared with all staff levels. (2 pts.) or (0 pts.)

4. Use and combine incentives with other strategies to increase participation in health promotion programs?

Answer "yes" if, for example, your organization offers incentives such as gift certificates, cash, paid time off, product or service discounts, reduced health insurance premiums, employee recognition, or prizes. (2 pts.) or (0 pts.)

5. Use competitions when combined with additional interventions to support employees making behavior changes?
Answer "yes" if, for example, your organization offers walking or weight loss competitions. (2 pts.) or (0 pts.)

6. Promote and market health promotion programs to employees?
Answer "yes" if, for example, your worksite's health promotion program has a brand name or logo, uses multiple channels of communication, or sends frequent messages. (1 pt.) or (0 pts.)

7. Use examples of employees role modeling appropriate health behaviors or employee health-related "success stories" in the marketing materials? (1 pt.) or (0 pts.)

8. Tailor some health promotion programs and education materials to the language, literacy levels, culture, or readiness to change of various segments of the workforce?

Answer "no" if you do not perceive a need for your organization to tailor its health promotion programs and education materials to any specific group(s). (3 pts.) or (0 pts.)

9. Have an active health promotion committee?

Answer "yes" if your health promotion committee exists and has been involved in planning and implementing programs. (2 pts.) or (0 pts.)

10. Have a paid health promotion coordinator whose job (either part-time or full-time) is to implement a worksite health promotion program?

Answer "yes" if implementing the employee health promotion program(s) at your worksite is included in a paid staff member's job description or performance expectations.
(2 pts.) or (0 pts.)

11. Have a champion(s) who is a strong advocate for the health promotion program?

Answer "yes" if there is someone at your worksite who actively promotes programs to improve worksite health promotion. (2 pts.) or (0 pts.)

12. Have an annual budget or receive dedicated funding for health promotion programs? (2 pts.) or (0 pts.)

13. Set annual organizational objectives for health promotion? (2 pts.) or (0 pts.)

14. Include references to improving or maintaining employee health in the business objectives or organizational mission statement?

Answer "no" if your organization's business objectives or mission statement only reference occupational health and safety, without reference to improving the workforce's health. (1 pt.) or (0 pts.)

15. Conduct ongoing evaluations of health promotion programming that use multiple data sources?

Answer "yes" if, for example, your organization collects data on employee health risks, medical claims, employee satisfaction, or organizational climate surveys. (2 pt.) or (0 pts.)

16. Make any health promotion programs available to family members? (1 pt.) or (0 pts.)

17. Provide flexible work scheduling policies?
Answer "yes" if, for example, policies allow for flextime schedules and work at home. (2 pts.) or (0 pts.)

18. Engage in other health initiatives throughout the community and support employee participation and volunteer efforts? Answer "yes "if, for example, your organization supports participation in community events and school-based efforts, such as corporate walks, collaborate with state and local advocacy groups, health and regulatory organizations, and coalitions. (2 pts.) or (0 pts.)

Your Worksite's Organizational Supports Section Score:
Maximum Organizational Supports Section Score: 33

Tobacco Control

During the past 12 months, did your worksite:

19. Have a written policy banning tobacco use at your worksite?
Answer "yes" if your worksite adheres to a statewide, countywide, or citywide policy banning tobacco use in the workplace. (3 pts.) or (0 pts.)

20. Actively enforce a written policy banning tobacco use?
Answer "yes" if, for example, your worksite posts signs, does not have ashtrays, or communicates this written policy banning tobacco use through various channels at your worksite.
(1 pt.) or (0 pts.)

21. Display signs (including 'no smoking' signs) with information about your tobacco-use policy? (1 pt.) or (0 pts.)

22. Refer tobacco users to a state or other tobacco cessation telephone quit line?

Answer "yes" if, for example, your worksite refers tobacco users to 1-800-QUIT NOW or smokefree.gov. (3 pts.) or (0 pts.)

23. Provide health insurance coverage with no or low out-of-pocket costs for prescription tobacco cessation medications including nicotine replacement?
Answer "yes" if, for example, your organization provides coverage for inhalers, nasal sprays, bupropion (e.g., Zyban) and varenicline (e.g.,Chantix). (3 pts.) or (0 pts.)

24. Provide health insurance coverage with no or low out-of-pocket costs for FDA-approved over-the-counter nicotine replacement products?

Answer "yes" if, for example, your organization provides coverage for nicotine replacement gum, patches, or lozenges.
(2 pts.) or (0 pts.)

25. Provide or promote free or subsidized tobacco cessation counseling?

Answer "yes" if these programs are provided on- or off-site; in group or individual settings; through vendors, on-site staff, health insurance plans or programs, community groups, or other practitioners. (2 pts.) or (0 pts.)

26. Inform employees about health insurance coverage or programs that include tobacco cessation medication and counseling? (2 pts.) or (0 pts.)

27. Provide incentives for being a current nonuser of tobacco and for current tobacco users that are currently involved in a cessation class or actively quitting?

Answer "yes" if, for example, your organization provides discounts on health insurance, or other benefits for non-smokers and tobacco users who are actively trying to quit. (1 pts.) or (0 pts.)

28. Do not allow sale of tobacco products on company property? Answer "yes" if, for example, your worksite does not sell tobacco products on company property in vending machines or through on-site vendors. (1 pt.) or (0 pts.)

Your Worksite's Tobacco Control Section Score: Maximum Tobacco Control Section Score: 19

Nutrition

During the past 12 months, did your worksite:

29. Provide places to purchase food and beverages?

Answer "yes" if, for example, your worksite provides vending machines, cafeterias, snack bars, or other purchase points. (Question not scored)

IF NO, PLEASE SKIP TO QUESTION 36.

30. Have a written policy or formal communication that makes healthier food and beverage choices available in cafeterias or snack bars?

Answer "yes" if, for example, the policy or formal communication makes vegetables, fruits, 100% fruit juices, whole grain items and trans fat-free or low-sodium snacks available in cafeterias or snack bars. (1 pt.) or (0 pts.)

31. Have a written policy or formal communication that makes

healthier food and beverage choices available in vending machines?

Answer "yes" if, for example, the policy or formal communication makes vegetables, fruits, 100% fruit juices, whole grain items and trans fat-free/low-sodium snacks available in vending machines. (1 pt.) or (0 pts.)

32. Make most (more than 50%) of the food and beverage choices available in vending machines, cafeterias, snack bars, or other purchase points be healthier food items?

Answer "yes" if the healthy foods are items such as skim milk, 1% milk, water, unsweetened flavored water, diet drinks, 100% fruit juice, low-fat and low-sodium snacks, or fresh fruit. (See Dietary Guidelines for Americans, 2010 or GSA/HHS Health and Sustainability Guidelines for Federal Concessions and Vending Operations.) (3 pts.) or (0 pts.)

33. Provide nutritional information (beyond standard nutrition information on labels) on sodium, calories, trans fats, or saturated fats for foods and beverages sold in worksite cafeterias, snack bars, or other purchase points? (2 pts.) or (0 pts.)

34. Identify healthier food and beverage choices with signs or symbols? ♥

Answer "yes" if, for example, your worksite puts a heart next to a healthy item near vending machines, cafeterias, snack bars, or other purchase points. (3 pts.) or (0 pts.)

35. Subsidize or provide discounts on healthier foods and beverages offered in vending machines, cafeterias, snack bars, or other purchase points? (3 pts.) or (0 pts.)

36. Have a written policy or formal communication which makes healthier food and beverage choices available during meetings when food is served?

Answer "yes" if, for example, the policy or formal communication makes vegetables, fruits, 100% fruit juices, whole grain items or trans fat-free/low-sodium snacks available during meetings. (1 pt.) or (0 pts.)

37. Provide employees with food preparation and storage facilities? Answer "yes" if your worksite provides a microwave oven, sink, refrigerator and/or

kitchen. (1 pt.) or (0 pts.)

38. Offer or promote an on-site or nearby farmers' market where fresh fruits and vegetables are sold? (1 pt.) (0 pts.)

39. Provide brochures, videos, posters, pamphlets, newsletters, or other written or online information that address the benefits of healthy eating?

Answer "yes" if these health promotion materials address the benefits of healthy eating as a single health topic or if the benefits of healthy eating are included with other health topics. (1 pt.) or (0 pts.)

40. Provide a series of educational seminars, workshops, or classes on nutrition?

Answer "yes" if these sessions address nutrition as a single health topic or if nutrition is included with other health topics. These sessions can be provided in-person or online; on-site or off-site; in group or individual settings; through vendors, on-site staff, health insurance plans or programs, community groups, or other practitioners. (2 pts.) or (0 pts.)

41. Provide free or subsidized self-management programs for healthy eating?

Answer "yes" if these programs are provided in-person or online; on-site or off-site; in group or individual settings; through vendors, on-site staff, health insurance plans and programs, community groups, or other practitioners. (2 pts.) or (0 pts.)

Your Worksite's Nutrition Section Score:
Maximum Nutrition Section Score: 21

Lactation Support

During the past 12 months, did your worksite:

42. Have a written policy on breastfeeding for employees?

Answer "yes" if the policy is included as a component of other employee policies or is a separate policy related to breastfeeding. (2 pts.) or (0 pts.)

43. Provide a private space (other than a restroom) that may be used by an employee to express breast milk? (3 pts.) or (0 pts.)

44. Provide access to a breast pump at the worksite? (3 pts.) or (0 pts.)

45. Provide flexible paid or unpaid break times to allow mothers to pump breast milk? (2 pts.) or (0 pts.)

46. Provide free or subsidized breastfeeding support groups or educational classes?

Answer "yes" if these sessions address breastfeeding as a single health topic or if breastfeeding is included with other health topics. These sessions can be provided in-person or online; onsite or offsite; in group or individual settings; through vendors, on-site staff, health insurance plans/programs, community groups, or other practitioners. (3 pts.) or (0 pts.)

47. Offer paid maternity leave, separate from any accrued sick leave, annual leave, or vacation time? (2 pts.) or (0 pts.)

Your Worksite's Lactation Support Section Score: Maximum Lactation Support Section Score: 15

Physical Activity

During the past 12 months, did your worksite:

48. Provide an exercise facility on-site? (3 pts.) or (0 pts.)

49. Subsidize or discount the cost of on-site or offsite exercise facilities? (3 pts.) or (0 pts.)

50. Provide environmental supports for recreation or physical activity?

Answer "yes" if, for example, your worksite provides trails or a track for walking/jogging, maps of suitable walking routes, bicycle racks, a basketball court, open space designated for recreation or exercise, a shower and changing facility. (3 pts.) or (0 pts.)

51. Post signs at elevators, stairwell entrances or exits and other key locations that encourage employees to use the stairs?
Answer "no" if your worksite is located in a one-story building. (3 pts.) or (0 pts.)

52. Provide organized individual or group physical activity programs

for employees (other than the use of an exercise facility)?

Answer "yes" if, for example, your worksite provides walking or stretching programs, group exercise, or weight training. (3 pts.) or (0 pts.)

53. Provide brochures, videos, posters, pamphlets, newsletters, or other written or online information that address the benefits of physical activity?

Answer "yes" if these health promotion materials address the benefits of physical activity as a single health topic or if the benefits of physical activity are included with other health topics. (1 pt.) or (0 pts.)

54. Provide a series of educational seminars, workshops, or classes on physical activity?

Answer "yes" if these sessions address physical activity as a single health topic or if physical activity is included with other health topics. These sessions can be provided in-person or online; on-site or off-site; in group or individual settings; through vendors, on-site staff, health insurance plans or programs, community groups, or other practitioners. (2 pts.) or (0 pts.)

55. Provide or subsidize physical fitness assessments, follow-up counseling, and physical activity recommendations either on-site or through a community exercise facility? (3 pts.) or (0 pts.)

56. Provide free or subsidized self-management programs for physical activity?

Answer "yes" if these programs are provided in-person or online; on-site or off-site; in group or individual settings; through vendors, on-site staff, health insurance plans or programs, community groups, or other practitioners. (3 pts.) or (0 pts.)

Your Worksite's Physical Activity Section Score:
Maximum Physical Activity Section Score: 24

Weight Management

During the past 12 months, did your worksite:

57. Provide free or subsidized body composition measurement, such as

height and weight, Body Mass Index (BMI) scores, or other body fat assessments (beyond self-report) followed by directed feedback and clinical referral when appropriate? (2 pts.) (0 pts.)

58. Provide brochures, videos, posters, pamphlets, newsletters, or other written or online information that address the risks of overweight or obesity?

Answer "yes" if these health promotion materials address the risks of overweight or obesity as a single health topic or if the risks of overweight or obesity are included with other health topics. (1 pt.) or (0 pts.)

59. Provide a series of educational seminars, workshops, or classes on weight management?

Answer "yes" if these sessions address weight management as a single health topic or if weight management is included with other health topics. These sessions can be provided in-person or online; on-site or off-site; in group or individual settings; through vendors, on-site staff, health insurance plans or programs, community groups, or other practitioners. (3 pts.) (0 pts.)

60. Provide free or subsidized one-on-one or group lifestyle counseling for employees who are overweight or obese?

Answer "yes" if these programs are provided in-person or online; on-site or off-site; in group or individual settings; through vendors, on-site staff, health insurance plans or programs, community groups, or other practitioners. (3 pts.) or (0 pts.)

61. Provide free or subsidized self-management programs for weight management?

Answer "yes" if these programs are provided in-person or online; on-site or off-site; in group or individual settings; through vendors, on-site staff, health insurance plans or programs, community groups, or other practitioners. (3 pts.) or (0 pts.)

Your Worksite's Weight Management Section Score:
Maximum Weight Management Section Score: 12

Stress Management

During the past 12 months, did your worksite:

62. Provide dedicated space that is quiet where employees can engage in relaxation activities, such as deep breathing exercises? (1 pt.) (0 pts.)

63. Sponsor or organize social events throughout the year?

Answer "yes" if, for example, your worksite sponsors or organizes team building events, company picnics, holiday parties, or employee sports teams. (1 pt.) (0 pts.)

64. Provide stress management programs?

Answer "yes" if these programs address stress management as a single health topic or if stress management is included with other health topics. Answer "yes" if these programs are provided in-person or online; on-site or off-site; in group or individual settings; through vendors, on-site staff, health insurance plans or programs, community groups, or other practitioners. (3 pts.) (0 pts.)

65. Provide work-life balance/ life-skills programs?

Answer "yes" if, for example, your worksite provides elder care, child care, referrals, tuition reimbursement, or other programs that are offered through vendors, on-site staff, or employee assistance programs. (3 pts.) (0 pts.)

66. Provide training for managers on identifying and reducing workplace stress-related issues?

Answer "yes" if, for example, your worksite provides training on performance reviews, communication, personnel management, assertiveness, time management, or conflict resolution. (3 pts.) (0 pts.)

67. Provide opportunities for employee participation in organizational decisions regarding workplace issues that affect job stress?

Answer "yes" if, for example, your worksite provides opportunities for employees to participate in decisions about work processes and environment, work schedules, participative problem-solving, and management of work demands. (3 pts.) (0 pts.)

Your Worksite's Stress Management Section Score:
Maximum Stress Management Section Score: 14

Depression

During the past 12 months, did your worksite:
68. Provide free or subsidized clinical screening for depression (beyond self-report) followed-by directed feedback and clinical referral when appropriate?

Answer "yes" if these services are provided directly through your organization or indirectly through a health insurance plan. (3 pts.) (0 pts.)

69. Provide access to online or paper self-assessment depression screening tools? (2 pts.) (0 pts.)

70. Provide brochures, videos, posters, pamphlets, newsletters, or other written or online information that address depression?

Answer "yes" if these health promotion materials address depression as a single health topic or if depression is included with other health topics. (2 pts.) (0 pts.)

71. Provide a series of educational seminars, workshops, or classes on preventing and treating depression?

Answer "yes" if these sessions address depression as a single health topic or if depression is included with other health topics. These sessions can be provided in-person or online; on-site or off-site; in group or individual settings; through vendors, on-site staff, health insurance plans or programs, community groups, or other practitioners. (3 pts.) (0 pts.)

72. Provide one-on-one or group lifestyle counseling for employees with depression?

Answer "yes" if these programs are provided in-person or online; onsite or off-site; in group or individual settings; through vendors, onsite staff, health insurance plans and programs, community groups, or other practitioners. (3 pts.) (0 pts.)

73. Provide training for managers on depression in the workplace?

Answer "yes" if, for example, your worksite provides managers with training on how to recognize depression, productivity or safety issues, and company or community resources for managing depression. (2 pts.) (0 pts.)

74. Provide health insurance coverage with no or low out-of-pocket costs for depression medications and mental health counseling? (3 pts.) (0 pts.)

Your Worksite's Depression Section Score:
Maximum Depression Section Score: 18

High Blood Pressure

During the past 12 months, did your worksite:

75. Provide free or subsidized blood pressure screening (beyond self-report) followed by directed feedback and clinical referral when appropriate? (3 pts.) (0 pts.)

76. Provide brochures, videos, posters, pamphlets, newsletters, or other written or online information that address the risks of high blood pressure?

Answer "yes" if these health promotion materials address the risks of high blood pressure as a single health topic or if the risks of high blood pressure are included with other health topics. (1 pt.) (0 pts.)

77. Provide a series of educational seminars, workshops, or classes on preventing and controlling high blood pressure?

Answer "yes" if these sessions address preventing or controlling high blood pressure as a single health topic or if preventing and controlling high blood pressure are included with other health topics.

These sessions can be provided in-person or online; on-site or offsite; in group or individual settings; through vendors, on-site staff, health insurance plans or programs, community groups, or other practitioners. (3 pts.) (0 pts.)

78. Provide one-on-one or group lifestyle counseling and follow-up monitoring for employees with high blood pressure or prehypertension?

Answer "yes" if these programs are provided in-person or online; on-site or off-site; in group or individual settings; through vendors, on-site staff, health insurance plans or programs, community groups, or other practitioners. (3 pts.) (0 pts.)

79. Provide free or subsidized self-management programs for blood pressure control and prevention?

Answer "yes" if these programs are provided in-person or online; on-site or off-site; in group or individual settings; through vendors, on-site staff, health insurance plans or programs, community groups, or other practitioners. (3 pts.) (0 pts.)

80. Make blood pressure monitoring devices available with instructions for employees to conduct their own self assessments? (2 pts.) (0 pts.)

81. Provide health insurance coverage with no or low out-of-pocket costs for blood pressure control medications? (2 pts.) (0 pts.)

Your Worksite's High Blood Pressure Section Score:
Maximum High Blood Pressure Section Score: 17

High Cholesterol

During the past 12 months, did your worksite:

82. Provide free or subsidized cholesterol screening (beyond self-report) followed by directed feedback and clinical referral when appropriate? (3 pts.) (0 pts.)

83. Provide brochures, videos, posters, pamphlets, newsletters, or other written or online information that address the risks of high cholesterol?

Answer "yes" if these health promotion materials address the risks of high cholesterol as a single health topic or if the risks of high cholesterol are included with other health topics. (1 pt.) (0 pts.)

84. Provide a series of educational seminars, workshops, or classes on preventing and controlling high cholesterol?

Answer "yes" if these sessions address preventing and controlling high cholesterol as a single health topic or if preventing and controlling high cholesterol are included with other health topics. These sessions can be provided in-person or online; on-site or off-site; in group or individual settings; through vendors, on-site staff, health insurance plans or programs, community groups, or other practitioners. (3 pts.) (0 pts.)

85. Provide one-on-one or group lifestyle counseling and follow-up monitoring for employees who have high cholesterol?

Answer "yes" if these programs are provided in-person or online; on-site or off-site; in group or individual settings; through vendors, on-site staff, health insurance plans or programs, community groups, or other practitioners. (3 pts.) (0 pts.)

86. Provide free or subsidized self-management programs for cholesterol or lipid control?

Answer "yes" if these programs are provided in-person or online; onsite or off-site; in group or individual settings; through vendors, onsite staff, health insurance plans and programs, community groups, or other practitioners. (3 pts.) (0 pts.)

87. Provide health insurance coverage no or low out-of-pocket costs for cholesterol or lipid control medications? (2 pts.) (0 pts.)

Your Worksite's High Cholesterol Section Score:
Maximum High Cholesterol Section Score: 15

Diabetes

During the past 12 months, did your worksite:

88. Provide free or subsidized pre-diabetes and diabetes risk factor assessment (beyond self-report) and feedback, followed by blood glucose screening and/or clinical referral when appropriate? (3 pts.) (0 pts.)

89. Provide brochures, videos, posters, pamphlets, newsletters, or other written or online information that address the risks of diabetes?

Answer "yes" if these health promotion materials address the risks of diabetes as a single health topic or if the risks of diabetes are included with other health topics. (1 pt.) (0 pts.)

90. Provide a series of educational seminars, workshops, or classes on preventing and controlling diabetes?

Answer "yes" if these sessions address preventing and controlling diabetes as a single health topic or if preventing and controlling diabetes are included with other health topics. These sessions can be provided in-person or online; on-site or off-site; in group or individual settings; through vendors, on-site staff, health insurance plans or programs, community groups, or other practitioners. (3 pts.) (0 pts.)

91. Provide one-on-one or group lifestyle counseling and follow-up monitoring for employees who have abnormal blood glucose levels (pre-diabetes or diabetes)?

Answer "yes" if these programs are provided in-person or online; on-site or off-site; in group or individual settings; through vendors, on-site staff, health insurance plans or programs, community groups, or other practitioners. (3 pts.) (0 pts.)

92. Provide free or subsidized self-management programs for diabetes control?

Answer "yes" if these programs are provided in-person or online; on-site or off-site; in group or individual settings; through vendors, on-site staff, health insurance plans or programs, community groups, or other practitioners. (3 pts.) (0 pts.)

93. Provide health insurance coverage with no or low out-ofpocket costs for diabetes medications and supplies for diabetes management (glucose test strips, needles, monitoring kits)? (2 pts.) (0 pts.)

Your Worksite's Diabetes Section Score:
Maximum Diabetes Section Score: 15

Signs and Symptoms of Heart Attack and Stroke

During the past 12 months, did your worksite:

94. Have posters or flyers in the common areas of your worksite (such

as bulletin boards, kiosks, break rooms) that identify the signs and symptoms of a heart attack and also convey that heart attacks are to be treated as emergencies? (1 pt.) (0 pts.)

95. Have posters or flyers in the common areas of your worksite (such as bulletin boards, kiosks, break rooms) that identify the signs and symptoms of a stroke and also convey that strokes are to be treated as emergencies? (1 pt.) (0 pts.)

96. Provide any other information on the signs and symptoms of heart attack through emails, newsletters, management communications, Web sites, seminars or classes? (1 pt.) (0 pts.)

97. Provide any other information on the signs and symptoms of stroke through e-mails, newsletters, management communications, Web sites, seminars or classes? (1 pt.) (0 pts.)

Your Worksite's Signs & Symptoms of Heart Attack, Stroke Section Score: Max. Signs and Symptoms of Heart Attack and Stroke Section Score: 4

Emergency Response to Heart Attack and Stroke

During the past 12 months, did your worksite:

98. Have an emergency response plan that addresses acute heart attack and stroke events? (2 pts.) (0 pts.)

99. Have an emergency response team for medical emergencies? (2 pts.) (0 pts.)

100. Offer access to a nationally-recognized training course on Cardiopulmonary Resuscitation (CPR) that includes training on Automated External Defibrillator (AED) usage? (3 pts.) (0 pts.)

101. Have a policy that requires an adequate number of employees per floor, work unit, or shift, in accordance with pertinent state and federal laws, to be certified in CPR/AED? (2 pts.) (0 pts.)

102. Have one or more functioning AEDs in place? IF NO, PLEASE SKIP TO QUESTION 107. (3 pts.) (0 pts.)

103. Have an adequate number of AED units such that a person can be reached within 3–5 minutes of collapse? (2 pts.) (0 pts.)

104. Identify the location of AEDS with posters, signs, markers, or other forms of communication other than on the AED itself? (1 pt.) (0 pts.)

105. Perform routine maintenance or testing on all AEDs? (1 pt.) (0 pts.)

106. Provide information to your local community Emergency Medical Service providers so they are aware that your worksite has an AED in place for an emergency response? (1 pt.) (0 pts.)

Your Worksite's Emergency Response to Heart Attack, Stroke Section Score:
Maximum Emergency Response to Heart Attack and Stroke Section Score: 17

Occupational Health and Safety

During the past 12 months, did your worksite:

107. Include improving or maintaining job health and safety in the business objectives or organizational mission statement?
Answer "yes" if any written vision, planning, or guideline documents include language about improving or maintaining worker health and safety. (1 pt.) (0 pts.)

108. Have a written injury and/or illness prevention program?
Answer "yes" if there is a written policy, whether or not it is posted. (2 pts.) (0 pts.)

109. Employ or contract for an occupational health and safety professional?

Answer "yes" if anyone is employed or contracted whose job includes improving health safety: example include occupational nurse, safety manager, environmental health manager, ergonomist, an insurance safety specialist who visits regularly. (3 pts.) (0 pts.)

110. Encourage reporting of injuries and near misses?
Answer "yes" if there is written and/or verbal encouragement to report injuries, illnesses, or near misses. (3 pts.) (0 pts.)

111. Provide opportunities for employee input on hazards and solutions? Answer "yes" if, for example, there were all-hands meetings,

196

tool box meetings, surveys, or focus groups for discovering and solving job health and/or safety issues. (3 pts.) (0 pts.)

112. Have a program to investigate the causes of injuries or illnesses?

Answer "yes" if, for example, there were all-hands meetings, tool box meetings, surveys, or focus groups for discovering and solving job health and/or safety issues. (3 pts.) (0 pts.)

113. Provide informational materials about health and safety at work to employees in most departments?

Answer "yes" if, for example, there are health and safety newsletters, fact sheets, posters, LED displays, emails, letters, broadcast messages, or other communications provided to employees. (1 pt.) (0 pts.) During the past 12 months, did your worksite: Yes No Score

114. Provide all new workers formal, comprehensive training on how to avoid accidents or injury on the job? (2 pts.) (0 pts.)

115. Coordinate programs for occupational health and safety with program for health promotion and wellness?

Answer "yes" if, for example a new safety initiative also includes a wellness component such as attention to diet, physical activity, smoking, etc.). (2 pts.) (0 pts.)

116. Have the following policies or benefits for employees been in place?

116A. Paid time off (PTO) for days or hours due to illness of employees or dependents (full-time, non-exempt employees).

[Note: non-exempt employees are those who are eligible to receive overtime pay if they work more than 40 hours in a week. Typically they are hourly workers.] (1 pt.) (0 pts.)

116B. Paid vacation time or personal days or hours to full-time, nonexempt employees). (1 pt.) (0 pts.)

Your Worksite's Occupational Health and Safety Section Score:
Maximum Occupational Health and Safety Section Score: 22

Vaccine-Preventable Diseases (VPD)

During the past 12 months, did your worksite:

117. Provide health insurance coverage with no or low out-of-pocket costs for influenza (flu) vaccination? (3 pts.) (0 pts.)

118. Provide health insurance coverage with no or low out-of-pocket costs for vaccinations other than influenza (flu) (e.g., pneumococcal or Tdap vaccines)? (3 pts.) (0 pts.)

119. Conduct influenza (flu) vaccinations at your worksite?

Answer "yes" if these offerings happen one or more times a year; are set up as either a temporary vaccine clinic run by an outside organization, internal occupational health staff or other arrangement.

IF NO, PLEASE PROCEED TO QUESTION NUMBER 121. (3 pts.) (0 pts.)

120. Provide influenza (flu) vaccinations at your worksite with no or low out-of-pocket costs to employees?

Answer "yes" if these offerings happen one or more times a year; are set up as either a temporary vaccine clinic run by an outside organization, internal occupational health staff or other arrangement. (3 pts.) (0 pts.)

121. Provide vaccinations other than seasonal influenza (e.g. pneumococcal or Tdap) at your worksite with no or low out-of pocket costs to employees?

Answer "yes" if these offerings happen one or more times a year; are set up as either a temporary vaccine clinic run by an outside organization, internal occupational health staff or other arrangement. (3 pts.) (0 pts.)

122. Promote influenza (flu) vaccinations through brochures, videos, posters, pamphlets, newsletters or other written or online information that address the benefits of influenza vaccinations?

Answer "yes" if these health promotion materials address the risks and benefits of influenza vaccination as a single health topic or if the benefits of influenza vaccinations are included with other health topics. (3 pts.) (0 pts.)

Your Worksite's Vaccine-Preventable Diseases Score:
Maximum Vaccine-Preventable Diseases Score: 18

Community Resources

During the past 12 months, did your worksite:

123. Provide employees with health related information, programs, or resources from any of the following organizations (not including your own organization)?

Respond "yes" or "no" to all questions. Answer "yes" if health information, programs, or resources are provided in-person or online; on-site or off-site; or in group or individual settings.

123A. State/local public health agency

123B. Health insurance plan

123C. Health management program and/or wellness program provider/vendor

123D. Workers compensation provider

123E. Health-related organizations (such as the American Heart Association, American Cancer Society, etc).

123F. Health insurance broker

123G. Hospital

123H. YMCA

123I. Community Organization or Business Group (Wellness Council, Chamber of Commerce or other business group)

123J. Other:

Respond "yes" if you work with an organization not listed above such as an Employee Assistance Program, Food Services, etc. to provide health information, programs, or resources to employees.

124. Receive consultation, guidance, advise, training, and/or direction from any of the following organizations related to the design and delivery of a worksite wellness program?

124A. State/local public health agency

124B. Health insurance plan

124C. Health management program and/or wellness program provider/vendor

124D. Workers compensation provider

124E. Health Related Organizations (such as the American Heart Association, American Cancer Society, etc).

124F. Health insurance broker

124G. Hospital

124H. YMCA

124I. Community or Business Organization (Wellness Council, Chamber of Commerce or other business group)

124J. Other:

Respond "yes" if you work with an organization not listed above such as an Employee Assistance Program, Food Services, etc. to provide health information, programs, or resources to employees.

125. Participate in any Community Coalitions focused on health or business and community partnerships?

END OF SURVEY

THANK YOU FOR COMPLETING THIS SURVEY!

Appendix 2: Definition of Terms

The following are definitions of terms that will be used throughout the study:

1. CDC Worksite Health Scorecard: "The CDC Worksite Health Scorecard (HSC) is a tool designed to help employers assess whether they have implemented evidence-based health promotion interventions or strategies in their worksites to prevent heart disease, stroke, and related conditions such as hypertension, diabetes, and obesity"(CDC, 2014).

2. Community resources for health and wellness: Providing employees with health related information, programs, or resources from a state or public health agency, a health insurance plan, or a workers compensation provider. This can also include support from a health management provider (onsite or a third party vendor), or support from an outside community resources such as the YMCA, a hospital, health insurance broker, or a wellness council, or chamber of commerce.

3. Depression support: Clinical screening for depression and directed feedback and clinical referral is an example of depression support by an organization. Depression support also includes educational literature, workshops, posters, videos, and group or lifestyle counseling for employees with depression.

4. Diabetes initiatives: Free or subsidized diabetes risk factor assessments. Organizational sponsored literature, videos, newsletters, educational seminars, lifestyle coaching, and self-management programs regarding the risk of diabetes. This can also include diabetes management devices and health insurance coverage with no or low out-of-pocket costs for glucose test strips, needles, monitoring kits, and other preventative measures.

5. Emergency response to heart attack and stroke mechanisms: An emergency response plan that addresses acute heart attack and stroke events, having an emergency response team, training on CPR. Additionally, having an automated external defibrillator (AED) onsite, maps to the nearest AED, and training and maintenance on AED devices.

6. High blood pressure related initiatives: Free or subsidized blood

pressure screening, beyond self-reporting. Organizational sponsored literature, videos, newsletters, educational seminars, lifestyle coaching, and self-management programs that support employees with high blood pressure. This can also include blood pressure monitoring devices and health insurance coverage with no or low out-of-pocket costs for blood pressure control medications and other preventative measures.

7. High cholesterol support: Free or subsidized cholesterol screening, feedback, clinical referral, educational material, lifestyle coaching, and insurance benefits for cholesterol or lipid control medication.

8. Lactation support: The act of employees being supported in breastfeeding by their organization. This includes having a written policy allowing employees time for breastfeeding, a designated space (other than a restroom) for breastfeeding, and a breast pump at the worksite. This allow can include unpaid break times to allow mothers to pump breast milk, breastfeeding support groups or classes, and even paid maternity leave for lactation.

9. Nutrition support: Organizational activities that encourage employees to make healthier food and beverage choices. These activities include policies, educational seminars, and formal communications that increase awareness and make healthier food choices available in vending machines, employee "pitch-ins", meetings, cafeterias, and snack bars. Nutrition support also includes signs or symbols on labels that indicate healthier food, providing discounts on healthier food, and giving employees food preparation and storage facilities.

10. Occupational health and safety presence: Job health and safety business objectives in the organizations mission statement or policy book, a written injury or illness prevention plan, and an employee or contractor who focuses on occupational health and safety. This also includes encouraging the reporting and investigation of injuries and near misses, as well as educational materials on how to prevent injuries and near misses.

11. Organizational supports: Human Resource and Leadership related mechanisms that provide assessments, health education, strategic incentives, dedicated labor, funding, and health promotion activities that are developed to improve employee health.

12. Physical activity engagement: This includes the many activities and mechanisms an organization can provide to encourage healthy, physical movement for their employees. This type of engagement includes an onsite gym or exercise facility, subsidized or discounted offsite exercise facilities, or environmental supports for recreation or physical activity. These environmental supports refer to worksite walking/jogging trials, bicycle racks, basketball courts, open spaces designed for exercise, and shower/changing facilities. They include educational services and policies that promote or explain the benefits of healthy physical activity. In best case scenarios, this includes assessments, follow-ups, and on-going programs for physical activity.

13. Signs and symptoms of heat attack and stroke materials: Posters or flyers in the common area of the workplace, emails, newsletters, or classes that help identify heart attack and stroke and alerting employees to treat them as emergencies.

14. Stress management: Stress management activities encourage employees to engage in relaxation activities, such as deep breathing, and allow a quiet space for employees to relax. Organizations can also organize social events, provide stress management programs, teach work-life balance, and help employees recognize stress-related issues.

15. Tobacco control: Organizational activities and policies that reduce or seek to eliminate the use of tobacco onsite and on the employee's own time. These activities can included policies, signage, tobacco cessation support services (such as training, a "quit line" telephone number, and financial incentives for tobacco cessation.

16. Vaccine-preventable disease programs: The organization providing onsite or no or low out-of-pocket costs for influenza and other vaccinations.

17. Weight management: Organizations can provide Body Mass Index scores or other body fat assessments, providing feedback and clinical referral if needed. This also includes educational services on obesity, one-on-one or group counseling, and free or subsidized programs for weight management.

18. Wellness: "Wellness is defined as a dynamic process of learning new life skills and becoming aware of and making conscious choices toward a more balanced and healthy lifestyle across seven dimensions: Social, Physical, Emotional, Career, Intellectual, Environmental, Spiritual (CDC, 2016).

19. Workplace wellness programs: "Workplace health programs are a coordinated and comprehensive set of health promotion and protection strategies implemented at the worksite that includes programs, policies, benefits, environmental supports, and links to the surrounding community designed to encourage the health and safety of all employees" (CDC, 2016).

Assumptions

This study operates with certain assumptions. First, the study presupposes that employers will continue to be providers of health insurance and thus bear a large cost of their employees' health care. As long as employers provide health insurance, they will have a stake in the cost of the health of their employees. Without paying for employees' health insurance, employers still have incentives for a healthy workforce, such as reduced absenteeism and greater productivity, but the financial pain of an unhealthy work force seems to be felt the most through providing health coverage.

The second assumption in this study is that employers are interested in reducing the costs of health care by making their employees healthier. It may be that employers do not care if the employees are healthy and these employers see disease and poor health as merely a cost of doing business. If this assumption is incorrect, then employers will ignore this study as they may be ignoring current literature on wellness. Even if employers are not interested in making their employees healthier, this study may persuade employers that the benefits of certain wellness programs are so compelling that employers will want to implement them.

Third, this study assumes that employers are willing to invest time, people, and money into workplace wellness programs to improve the health of their work force. Employers may want their workforce to be healthier. They may believe it is possible to see benefits from these programs, but they may not want to invest in these programs. When exploring short and long-term improvement strategies, such as training and education, investment in infrastructure, or retaining a workforce in an economic downturn, it can be difficult for employers to see the long-range benefits of employee health and wellness. Leaders can be tempted to think in the short-term and not be willing to spend a dollar today to save three to five dollars in five to ten years.

Fourth, the study will use the Centers for Disease Control health scorecard to guide the research. This assumes that the CDC HSC is a reliable tool for determining the health of a workplace. Researchers at Emory University conducted validation studies to prove that this scorecard is a worthwhile instrument for determining workplace wellness. Since the study relies on the scorecard for gathering both quantitative and qualitative data, the study assumes the scorecard is valid.

The fifth assumption of the study is that participants of the study are willing and able to answer the CDC scorecard and follow-up questions honestly. This implies that they have access to the knowledge and can share it. Preliminary research suggests that the costs and benefits of wellness programs are not extensively tracked. The use of the quantitative score of the CDC scorecard and the qualitative questions is an attempt to use an objective instrument to gather as much information as possible.

The final assumption we will discuss is the assumption that employers are not already doing everything they can to improve workplace wellness. If employers are already doing everything they can and are at the limit of their "wellness bandwidth", then nothing more can be done for work place wellness. This assumption seems fair based on preliminary research that tells us that many employers are not participating in workplace wellness, they are just getting started, or they may have programs but their employee participation is poor.

Limitations

There are limitations to this study and those are investigated in this section. The study's procedures ensure that the limitations are minimized, but they are not eliminated. The study investigates participants from the technology industry that hire students from Purdue Polytechnic New Albany. The first limitation is that those attending the 2017 career fair will not want to participate in the study. If this is the case, then a sample of convenience may be necessary. The sample of convenience is not ideal because it only includes those participants that are easy to reach. A sample of convenience can skew the results toward a certain profile; such as those that know the author or those that are eager to participate in a study, because they are strong (or weak) in wellness programs.

Another limitation of the study is that by using the CDC scorecard, the results of the findings are only as good as the instrument itself. There are a variety of wellness instruments that could be used to study wellness programs in the population. The literature review in Chapter Two will explore these various wellness-measuring instruments. Additionally, the aforementioned study by researchers at Emory University validated and improved the CDC scorecard. Their research will be included to address this limitation.

Time is another limitation in this study. Interviewing and surveying organizational leaders in person is time consuming and does not allow us to speak with that many members in-depth. Therefore, the population needs to be representative enough to provide reasonable conclusions. Time is also a limitation because the study only provides a snapshot at a given time and circumstances can change for the participants. The study will acknowledge this limitation and attempt to set the stage for further research by determining the wellness factors that employers can address over the next five years. The study first examines initiatives for the most pressing concerns.

The final limitation to mention in this section is that workplace wellness programs can be a subject many employers may want to keep confidential. First, they may see their program as a competitive advantage and/or proprietary information that they do not want to share. Second, they may see their lack of a wellness program as an embarrassment and do not want the public to know they are falling short in this area. Therefore, confidentially is promised and ensured in order to obtain authentic feedback from the leaders included in the study. A way to maintain anonymity is to describe an organization as "a $100 million per year manufacturer, with 500-600 employees." The study includes the Institutional Review Board to meet ethical standards in research.

REFERENCES

Allexandre, D., Bernstein, A. M., Walker, E., Hunter, J., Roizen, M. F., & Morledge, T. J. (2016). A Web-Based Mindfulness Stress Management Program in a Corporate Call Center. *Journal of Occupational & Environmental Medicine, 58*(3), 254-264. doi:10.1097/JOM.0000000000000680

Allin, S., Busse, R., Durán, A., Evans, D., Figueras, J, Dr., Karanikolos, M., ... Wismar, M. (2012). *Health systems, health, wealth and societal well-being: Assessing the case for investing in health systems [PDF Version].*

Alyssa B. Schultz, D. W. E. (2007). Employee Health and Presenteeism: A Systematic

Review. *J Occup Rehabil, 17:547–579.*

Arena, R., Guazzi, M., Briggs, P. D., Cahalin, L. P., Myers, J., Kaminsky, L. A., ... Lavie, C. J. (2013). Promoting health and wellness in the workplace: a unique opportunity to establish primary and extended secondary cardiovascular risk reduction programs. *Mayo Clinic Proceedings, 88*(6), 605-617. doi:10.1016/j.mayocp.2013.03.002

Baicker, K., Cutler, D., & Zirui, S. (2010). Workplace Wellness Programs Can Generate Savings. *Health Affairs, 29*(2), 1-8. doi:10.1377/hlthaff.2009.0626

Baskin, E., Gorlin, M., Chance, Z., Novemsky, N., Dhar, R., Huskey, K., & Hatzis, M. (2016). Proximity of snacks to beverages increases food consumption in the workplace: A field study. *Appetite, 103*, 244-248. doi:10.1016/j.appet.2016.04.025

Belay, B., Allen, J., Williams, N., Dooyema, C., & Foltz, J. (2013). Promoting Women's Health in Hospitals: A Focus on Breastfeeding and Lactation Support for Employees and Patients. *Journal of Women's Health (15409996), 22*(1), 1-4. doi:10.1089/jwh.2012.4040

Benz, J., Sedensky, M., Tompson, T., & Agiesta, J. (2013). *Working longer: Older Americans' attitudes on work and retirement.* Chicago: NORC Center for Public Affairs Research Retrieved from www.apnorc.org/projects/Pages/ working-longer-older-americans-attitudes-on-work-and-retirement.aspx.

Blake, H., & Lee, S. (2007). Health of community nurses: a case for workplace wellness schemes. *British Journal of Community Nursing, 12*(6), 263-267.

Blumberg, A. D. (2009). *Accidents of history created U.S. health system.* National Public Radio: All things considered. Retrieved from http://www.npr.org/templates/story/story.php?storyId=114045132

Boardley, D., & Pobocik, R. S. (2009). Obesity on the rise. *Primary Care, 36*(2), 243-255. doi:10.1016/j.pop.2009.01.003

Borovoy, A., & Roberto, C. A. (2015). Japanese and American public health approaches to preventing population weight gain: A role for paternalism? *Social Science & Medicine, 143*, 62-70. doi:10.1016/j.socscimed.2015.08.018

Caban-Martinez, A. J., Davila, E. P., McCollister, K. E., Fleming, L. E., Zheng, D. D., Lam, B. L., . . . Lee, D. J. (2011). Age-related macular degeneration and smoking cessation advice by eye care providers: A pilot study. *Preventing Chronic Disease, 8*(6).

California Department of Public Health, N. E. a. O. P. B. (2015). *Worksite program success stories: Creating a culture of wellness in the worksite environment.* Retrieved from https://www.cdph.ca.gov/programs/cpns/Documents/300201_Worksit eSuccessStories_LowRes.pdf.

Cavallo, D. N., Tate, D. F., Ries, A. V., Brown, J. D., DeVellis, R. F., & Ammerman, A. S. (2012). A social media-based physical activity intervention: a randomized controlled trial. *American Journal of Preventive Medicine, 43*(5), 527-532.

CDC. (2008). *Smoking-attributal mortality, years of potential life lost, and productivity losses— United States, 2000—2004.*

CDC. (2011). *National diabetes fact sheet: National estimates and general information on diabetes and pre-diabetes in the United States.* Atlanta, GA.

CDC. (2014). *The CDC worksite health scorecard: An assessment tool for employers to prevent heart disease, stroke, and related health conditions.* Retrieved from http://www.cdc.gov/dhdsp/pubs/docs/hsc_manual.pdf.

CDC. (2016). *Workplace health program definition and description.* Retrieved from https://www.cdc.gov/workplacehealthpromotion/pdf/workplace-health-program-definition-and-description.pdf.

Chance, Z., Gorlin, M., & Dhar, R. (2014). Why Choosing Healthy Foods is Hard, and How to Help: Presenting the 4Ps Framework for Behavior Change. *Customer Needs and Solutions, 1*(4), 253-262.

Chapman, L. S. (2012). Meta-Evaluation of Worksite Health Promotion Economic Return Studies: 2012 Update. *American Journal of Health Promotion, 26*(4), TAHP.1-TAHP.10. doi:10.4278/ajhp.26.4.tahp

Chehimi, S., Cohen, L., & Valdovinos, E. (2011). In the first place: community prevention's promise to advance health and equity. *Environment & Urbanization, 23*(1), 71-89. doi:10.1177/0956247811398600

Commission, U. S. E. E. O. (2016a). *EEOC's final rule on employer wellness programs and the genetic information nondiscrimination act.* Retrieved from https://www.eeoc.gov/laws/regulations/qanda-gina-wellness-final-rule.cfm.

Commission, U. S. E. E. O. (2016b). *EEOC's final rule on employer wellness programs and title I of the Americans with disabilities act.* . Retrieved from https://www.eeoc.gov/laws/regulations/qanda-ada-wellness-final-rule.cfm.

Committee, O. S. I. H. a. W. (2016). [Committee Meeting].

Cropanzano, R., & Mitchell, M. S. (2005). Social Exchange Theory: An Interdisciplinary Review. *Journal of Management, 31*(6), 874-900.

Davis, K., Stremikis, K., Squires, D., & Schoen, C. (2014). *Mirror, mirror on the wall, 2014 update: How the performance of the U.S. health care system compares internationally.* Retrieved from The Commonwealth Fund http://www.commonwealthfund.org/publications/fund-reports/2014/jun/mirror-mirror

De Libero, F. (2013). A fresh look at health care cost growth. Retrieved from http://www.lettingthedataspeak.com/a-fresh-look-at-health-care-cost-growth/

Dee W. Edington, A. B. S., Jennifer S. Pitts. (2015). *Population Health: Creating a Culture of Wellness* (J. R. David B. Nash, Raymond J. Fabius, Janice L. Clarke, Alexis Skoufalos Ed.). Burlington, MA: Jones and Bartlett.

DeVries, G. (2010). Innovations in Workplace Wellness: Six New Tools to Enhance Programs and Maximize Employee Health and Productivity. *Compensation & Benefits Review, 42*(1), 46-51.

Drezner, J. A., Courson, R. W., Roberts, W. O., Mosesso Jr, V. N., Link, M. S., & Maron, B. J. (2007). Inter-Association Task Force Recommendations on Emergency Preparedness and Management of Sudden Cardiac Arrest in High School and College Athletic Programs: A Consensus Statement. *Journal of Athletic Training (National Athletic Trainers' Association), 42*(1), 143-158.

Duijts, L., Jaddoe, V. W. V., Hofman, A., & Moll, H. A. (2010). Prolonged and exclusive breastfeeding reduces the risk of infectious diseases in infancy. *Pediatrics, 126*(1), e18-e25. doi:10.1542/peds.2008-3256

Edington, D. W., Schultz, A. B., Pitts, J. S., & Camilleri, A. (2016). The Future of Health Promotion in the 21st Century. *American Journal of Lifestyle Medicine, 10*(4), 242-252. doi:doi:10.1177/1559827615605789

EEOC. (2011). *Informal Discussion Letter, ADA & GINA: incentives for workplace wellness programs.* Retrieved from http://www.ee oc.gov/eeoc/foia/letters/2011/ada_gina_incentives.html.

Finkelstein, E. A., Trogdon, J. G., Cohen, J. W., & Dietz, W. (2009). Annual Medical Spending Attributable To Obesity: Payer- And Service-Specific Estimates. *Health Affairs, 28,* w822-w831. doi:10.1377/hlthaff.28.5.w822

Foundation, P. G. P. (2016). *United States per capita healthcare spending is more than twice the average of other developed countries.* . Retrieved from http://www.pgpf.org/chart-archive/0006_health-care-oecd

Frank, R. H. (2008). Nudge: Improving Decisions about Health, Wealth, and Happiness. *Ethics, 119*(1), 202-208.

French, S. A. (2003). Pricing Effects on Food Choices. *Journal of Nutrition, 133*(3), 841S-843S.

Goetzel, R. Z., Henke, R. M., Tabrizi, M., Pelletier, K. R., Loeppke, R., Ballard, D. W., . . . Exum, E. (2014). Do Workplace Health Promotion (Wellness) Programs Work? *Journal of Occupational & Environmental Medicine, 56*(9), 927-934. doi:10.1097/JOM.0000000000000276

Goetzel, R. Z., & Ozminkowski, R. J. (2008). The Health and Cost Benefits of Work Site Health-Promotion Programs. *Annual Review of Public Health, 29*(1), 303-223. doi:10.1146/annurev.publhealth.29.020907.090930

Goldman, L. S., Nielsen, N. H., & Champion, H. C. (1999). Awareness, Diagnosis, and Treatment of Depression. *JGIM: Journal of General Internal Medicine, 14*(9), 569-580. doi:10.1046/j.1525-1497.1999.03478.x

Goodman, A. K., Friedman, S. M., Beatrice, S. T., & Bart, S. W. (1987). Rubella in the workplace: the need for employee immunization. *American journal of public health, 77*(6), 725-726.

Green, D. P., Fox, J. (2007). *Rational choice theory*: Sage.

Heidenreich, P. A., Trogdon, J. G., Khavjou, O. A., Butler, J., Dracup, K., Ezekowitz, M. D., . . . Outcomes, R. (2011). Forecasting the future of cardiovascular disease in the United States: a policy statement from the American Heart Association. *Circulation, 123*(8), 933-944.

Herbert, W. G., Herbert, D. L., McInnis, K. J., Ribisl, P. M., Franklin, B. A., Callahan, M., & Hood, A. W. (2007). Cardiovascular emergency preparedness in recreation facilities at major US universities: college fitness center emergency readiness. *Preventive cardiology, 10*(3), 128-133.

Horacek, T. M., White, A. A., Byrd-Bredbenner, C., Reznar, M. M., Olfert, M. D., Morrell, J. S., . . . Thompson-Snyder, C. A. (2014). PACES: a Physical Activity Campus Environmental Supports Audit on university campuses. *American Journal Of Health Promotion: AJHP, 28*(4), e104-e117. doi:10.4278/ajhp.121212-QUAN-604

Hughes, M. C., Hannon, P. A., Harris, J. R., & Patrick, D. L. (2010). Health Behaviors of Employed and Insured Adults in the United States, 2004--2005. *American Journal of Health Promotion, 24*(5), 315-323.

Hughes, M. C., Yette, E. M., Hannon, P. A., Harris, J. R., Tran, N. M., & Reid, T. R. (2011). Promoting tobacco cessation via the workplace: opportunities for improvement. *Tobacco Control, 20*(4), 305-308. doi:10.1136/tc.2010.041038

Hyatt Neville, B., Merrill, R. M., & Kumpfer, K. L. (2011). Longitudinal Outcomes of a Comprehensive, Incentivized Worksite Wellness Program. *Evaluation & the Health Professions, 34*(1), 103-123. doi:10.1177/0163278710379222

Hymel, P. A., Loeppke, R. R., Baase, C. M., Burton, W. N., Hartenbaum, N. P., Hudson, T. W., . . . Larson, P. W. (2011). Workplace health protection and promotion: a new pathway for a healthier--and safer--workforce. *Journal Of Occupational And Environmental Medicine, 53*(6), 695-702. doi:10.1097/JOM.0b013e31822005d0

Ip, S., Chung, M., Raman, G., Chew, P., Magula, N., DeVine, D., . . . Lau, J. (2007). Breastfeeding and maternal and infant health outcomes in developed countries. *Evidence Report/Technology Assessment*(153), 1-186.

Jackson, J., Kohn-Parrott, K. A., Parker, C., Levins, N., Dyer, S., Hedalen, E. J., . . . Doyle, J. J. (2011). Blood Pressure Success Zone: You Auto Know. A worksite-based program to improve blood pressure control among auto workers. *Population health management, 14*(5), 257-263.

John, E. J., Vavra, T., Farris, K., Currie, J., Doucette, W., Button-Neumann, B., . . . Bullock, T. (2006). Workplace-Based Cardiovascular Risk Management by Community Pharmacists: Impact on Blood Pressure, Lipid Levels, and Weight. *Pharmacotherapy, 26*(10), 1511-1517.

Joslin, B., Lowe, J. B., & Peterson, N. A. (2006). Employee Characteristics and Participation in a Worksite Wellness Programme. *Health Education Journal, 65*(4), 308-319.

Kahn, E. B., Ramsey, L. T., Brownson, R. C., Heath, G. W., Howze, E. H., Powell, K. E., . . . Blood Institute, N. I. o. H. B. M. U. S. A. (2002). The effectiveness of interventions to increase physical activity:A systematic review 1,2 1 The names and affiliations of the Task Force members are listed in the front of this supplement and at www.thecommunityguide.org. 2 Address correspondence and reprint requests to: Peter A. Briss, MD, Community Guide Branch, Centers for Disease Control and Prevention, 4770 Buford Highway, MS-K73, Atlanta, GA 30341. E-mail: PBriss@cdc.gov. *American Journal of Preventive Medicine: Supplement 1, 22*(4 Supplement 1), 73-107.

Kent, K., Goetzel, R. Z., Roemer, E. C., Prasad, A., & Freundlich, N. (2016). Promoting Healthy Workplaces by Building Cultures of Health and Applying Strategic Communications. *Journal Of Occupational And Environmental Medicine, 58*(2), 114-122. doi:10.1097/JOM.0000000000000629

King, A. C. (1998). How to promote physical activity in a community: research experiences from the US highlighting different community approaches. *PATIENT EDUCATION AND COUNSELING, 33 SUPP/1*, S3-S12.

Break time for nursing mothers, (2012).

Light, E. M. W., Kline, A. S., Drosky, M. A., & Chapman, L. S. (2015). Economic Analysis of the Return-on-Investment of a Worksite Wellness Program for a Large Multistate Retail Grocery Organization. *Journal Of Occupational And Environmental Medicine, 57*(8), 882-892.

Lind, K. D., & Noel-Miller. (2011). Chronic condition prevalence in the 50+ US population. In AARP (Ed.), *Fact Sheet No. 245*. Washington, DC.

Linnan, L., Weiner, B., Graham, A., & Emmons, K. (2007). Manager Beliefs Regarding Worksite Health Promotion: Findings From the Working Healthy Project 2. *American Journal of Health Promotion, 21*(6), 521-528.

Liu, Y.-H., Huang, L.-M., & Wang, J.-D. (2004). Reduction of acute respiratory illness (ARI) due to a voluntary workplace influenza vaccination program: who are more likely to get the benefit? *Journal Of Occupational Health, 46*(6), 455-460.

Luckhaupt, S. E., Cohen, M. A., Li, J., & Calvert, G. M. (2014). Prevalence of Obesity Among U.S. Workers and Associations with Occupational Factors. *American Journal of Preventive Medicine, 46*(_3), 237-248. doi:10.1016/j.amepre.2013.11.002

MacDonald, S. C., & Westover, J. H. (2011). The Impact of Workplace Wellness Programs on Decreasing Employee Obesity and Increasing Overall Health. *Journal of the Utah Academy of Sciences, Arts & Letters, 88*, 91-113.

Medicine, J. H. S. o. (2003). Definition of De-Identified Data. Retrieved from http://www.hopkinsmedicine.org/institutional_review_board/hipaa_rese arch/de_identified_data.html

Mello, M. M., & Rosenthal, M. B. (2008). Wellness Programs and Lifestyle Discrimination — The Legal Limits. *New England Journal of Medicine, 359*(2), 192-199. doi:10.1056/NEJMhle0801929

Merrill, R. M., Aldana, S. G., Garrett, J., & Ross, C. (2011). Effectiveness of a Workplace Wellness Program for Maintaining Health and Promoting Healthy Behaviors. *Journal of Occupational & Environmental Medicine, 53*(7), 782-787. doi:10.1097/JOM.0b013e318220c2f4

Mhurchu, C. N., Aston, L. M., & Jebb, S. A. (2010). Effects of worksite health promotion interventions on employee diets: a systematic review. *BMC Public Health, 10*(1), 1-7. doi:10.1186/1471-2458-10-62

Milani, R. V., & Lavie, C. J. (2009). Impact of Worksite Wellness Intervention on Cardiac Risk Factors and One-Year Health Care Costs. *American Journal of Cardiology, 104*(10), 1389-1392. doi:10.1016/j.amjcard.2009.07.007

Miller, S. (2015). *Employer's health costs projected to rise 6.5% for 2016: Making plan design changes could reduce increase to 4.5%.* . Retrieved from https://www.shrm.org/ResourcesAndTools/hr-topics/benefits/Pages/health-cost-forecast-2016.aspx

Moseley, K., & Estrada-Portales, I. M. (2013). RAND Report on Workplace Wellness: what employers must know. *Population health management, 16*(5), 349-350.

Murray, C. J. L., & Lopez, A. D. (1996). Evidence-based health policy--lessons from the Global Burden of Disease Study. *Science, 274*(5288), 740.

Ortiz, J., McGilligan, K., & Kelly, P. (2004). Duration of Breast Milk Expression Among Working Mothers Enrolled in an Employer-Sponsored Lactation Program. *Pediatric Nursing, 30*(2), 111-119.

Park, S., Pan, L., & Lankford, T. (2014). Relationship between employment characteristics and obesity among employed U.S. adults. *American Journal of Health Promotion, 28*(6), 389-396.

Pollitz, K. R., M. (2016). *Workplace wellness programs characteristics and requirements.* Retrieved from http://kff.org/private-insurance/issue-brief/workplace-wellness-programs-characteristics-and-requirements/

Pomeranz, J. L. (2015). Participatory Workplace Wellness Programs: Reward, Penalty, and Regulatory Conflict. *Milbank Quarterly, 93*(2), 301-318. doi:10.1111/1468-0009.12123

Richardsen, A. M., & Burke, R. J. (2014). Corporate wellness programs: A summary of best practices and effectiveness. In R. J. Burke, A. M. Richardsen, R. J. Burke, & A. M. Richardsen (Eds.), *Corporate wellness programs: Linking employee and organizational health.* (pp. 349-365). Northampton, MA, US: Edward Elgar Publishing.

Roger, V. L., Go, A. S., Lloyd-Jones, D. M., Benjamin, E. J., Berry, J. D., Borden, W. B., . . . Stroke Statistics, S. (2012). Heart disease and stroke statistics-- 2012 update: a report from the American Heart Association. *Circulation, 125*(1), e2-e220.

Sallis, J., Bauman, A., Pratt, M. C. f. D. C., & Prevention, A. G. U. S. A. (1998). Environmental and policy interventions to promote physical activity a a This work was prepared for the CIAR Conference on Physical Activity Promotion: An ACSM Specialty Conference. *American Journal of Preventive Medicine, 15*(4), 379-397.

Schonfeld, I. S., & Bianchi, R. (2016). Burnout and Depression: Two Entities or One? *Journal of Clinical Psychology, 72*(1), 22-37. doi:10.1002/jclp.22229

Scott, J. (2000). *Rational Choice Theory:* Sage Publications.

Services, U. D. o. H. a. H. (2000). *Healthy People 2010, With Understanding and Improving Health and Objectives for Improving Health.* Washington, D.C. Retrieved from http://www.healthypeople.gov/2010/Document/HTML/Volume1/07E d.htm# Toc490550857.

Services, U. S. D. o. H. a. H. (2007). *The effect of health care cost growth on the U.S. economy (Final Report for Task Order # HP-06-12).* Retrieved from https://aspe.hhs.gov/sites/default/files/pdf/75441/report.pdf.

Services, U. S. D. o. H. a. H. (2012). *HIPAA privacy and security and workplace wellness programs.* Retrieved from http://www.hhs.gov/hipaa/for-professionals/privacy/workplace-wellness/.

Services, U. S. D. o. H. a. H. (2014). *Medical expenditure panel survey* Retrieved from https://meps.ahrq.gov/mepsweb/data_stats/quick_tables_results.jsp?co

mponent=2&subcomponent=2&year=2014&tableSeries=1&tableSubSeri
es=CDE&searchText=&searchMethod=1&Action=Search.

Slootmaker, S. M., Schuit, A. J., Chinapaw, M. J. M., Seidell, J. C., & Van Mechelen, W. (2009). Disagreement in physical activity assessed by accelerometer and self-report in subgroups of age, gender, education and weight status. *International Journal of Behavioral Nutrition & Physical Activity, 6*, 1-10. doi:10.1186/1479-5868-6-17

Soárez, P. C. d., Ciconelli, R. M., Pavin, T., Ogata, A. J. N., Curci, K. A., & Oliveira, M. R. d. (2016). Cross-cultural adaptation of the CDC Worksite Health ScoreCard questionnaire into Portuguese. *Revista Da Associacao Medica Brasileira (1992), 62*(3), 236-242. doi:10.1590/1806-9282.62.03.236

Sohyun, P., Liping, P., & Lankford, T. (2014). Relationship Between Employment Characteristics and Obesity Among Employed U.S. Adults. *American Journal of Health Promotion, 28*(6), 389-396. doi:10.4278/ajhp.130207-QUAN-64

Stampfer, M. J., Hu, F. B., & Willett, W. C. (2000). Primary Prevention of Coronary Heart Disease in Women through Diet and Lifestyle (Vol. 343, pp. 1814-1815).

Terry, P. E. (2013). The Science Stalwarts for Wellness: The CDC (and P). *American Journal of Health Promotion, 28*(2).

Thorpe, K. E., Florence, C. S., Howard, D. H., & Joski, P. (2004). The Impact Of Obesity On Rising Medical Spending. *Health Affairs, 23*, 480-486. doi:10.1377/hlthaffW4.480

Toland, B. (2014, 4/27/2014). How did America end up with this health care system? *Pittsburgh Post Gazette.*

U.S. Department of Labor, B. o. L. S. (2014). *Fact sheet: The affordable care act and wellness programs.* Retrieved from https://www.dol.gov/ebsa/newsroom/fswellnessprogram.html.

U.S. Department of Labor, B. o. L. S. (2016a). *Local area unemployment statistics.* . Retrieved from http://www.bls.gov/web/laus/laumstrk.htm.

U.S. Department of Labor, B. o. L. S. (2016b). *News release: Employer costs for employee compensation - March 2016 (USDL-16-1150).* Retrieved from http://www.bls.gov/news.release/pdf/ecec.pdf.

U.S. Department of Labor, B. o. L. S. (2016c). *News Release: The Employment Situation-June 2016.* Retrieved from http://www.bls.gov/news.release/pdf/empsit.pdf.

VanderVeur, J., Gilchrist, S., & Matson-Koffman, D. (2015). An Overview of State Policies Supporting Worksite Health Promotion Programs. *American Journal of Health Promotion, 31*(3), 232-242.

Weiss, J. P., Froelicher, V. F., Myers, J. N., & Heidenreich, P. A. (2004). Health-Care Costs and Exercise Capacity. *CHEST, 126*(2), 608-613.

White, M. J., Loccoh, E. C., Goble, M. M., Yu, S., Duquette, D., Davis, M. M., . . . Communicable Diseases, U. o. M. A. A. M. I. (2016). Availability of Automated External Defibrillators in Public High Schools. *The Journal of Pediatrics, 172*, 142-146.e141.

Witt, D. D., Dr. (2013). *Five major theories: Social exchange theory and developmental theories.* University of Akron Website. Retrieved from http://www3.uakron.edu/witt/fc/fcnote5b.htm

Wong, N. D., Lopez, V. A., L'Italien, G., Chen, R., Kline, S. E. J., & Franklin, S. S. (2007). Inadequate Control of Hypertension in US Adults With Cardiovascular Disease Comorbidities in 2003-2004. *Archives of Internal Medicine, 167*(22), 2431-2436.

Yin, R. K. (2009). *Case Study Research* (Fourth Edition ed.). Thousand Oaks, California: SAGE.

Young-Ybarra, C., & Wiersema, M. (1999). Strategic Flexibility in Information Technology Alliances: The Influence of Transaction Cost Economics and Social Exchange Theory. *Organization Science, 10*(4), 439-459. Retrieved from

ABOUT THE AUTHOR

Andrew L. McCart grew up in Orleans, Indiana, "a town of 2,000 friendly folks." In academia, he completed a Doctor of Philosophy in Public Health at the University of Louisville, and Master's and Bachelor's degrees of Business Administration at Indiana University. Andrew has been a professor of Organizational Leadership, Entrepreneurship, and Industrial Engineering Technology at Purdue University. He is a Senior Instructor with the Healing Tao Instructor Association of the Americas. He holds three black belts in martial arts and studies various healing modalities, including Chi Nei Tsang, Reiki, Acupressure, Cosmic Healing Chi Kung, and Medical Chi Kung. His hobbies include CrossFit, martial arts, coffee, and travel. He lives in the Louisville, Kentucky area with his wife Deven, their Siberian Husky "Sugar" and sometimes his parents' dog "Katie.". Please follow him on his website, The Tao Blog, and various social media platforms. Here he provides videos, teachings, and info on health-related topics.

Made in the USA
Monee, IL
18 July 2020